Unique Challenges in Urban Schools

Unique Challenges in Urban Schools

The Involvement of African American Parents

Eric Jackson, Carolyn Turner,
and Dorothy E. Battle

ROWMAN & LITTLEFIELD
Lanham • Boulder • New York • London

Published by Rowman & Littlefield
A wholly owned subsidiary of The Rowman & Littlefield Publishing Group, Inc.
4501 Forbes Boulevard, Suite 200, Lanham, Maryland 20706
www.rowman.com

Unit A, Whitacre Mews, 26-34 Stannary Street, London SE11 4AB

Library of Congress Cataloging-in-Publication Data Available

ISBN 978-1-61048-008-6 (cloth : alk. paper) -- ISBN 978-1-61048-009-3 (pbk. : alk. paper) -- ISBN 978-1-61048-010-9 (electronic)

∞ ™ The paper used in this publication meets the minimum requirements of American National Standard for Information Sciences Permanence of Paper for Printed Library Materials, ANSI/NISO Z39.48-1992.

Printed in the United States of America

Table of Contents

Acknowledgments

We would not have completed this project without the encouragement, support, and assistance of numerous individuals. We are greatly indebted and give much thanks to our editor Thomas F. Koerner. His patience, understanding, and vision deeply inspired us to continue in the process despite its many trials and tribulations. There is no question that without him, this book would not have been published with such precision and care.

There are many other people and institutions we also wish to thank for their valuable contributions to the research and completion of this book. We always will be thankful to Kevin Grace at Blegan Library, the library staff at Langsam Library at the University of Cincinnati, and the folks at the W. Frank Steely Library at Northern Kentucky University. A great amount of the research contained in this volume came from these outstanding research facilities.

We wish to thank all the parents, educators, and other professionals whose experiences greatly enhanced this project. The names were changed to protect their anonymity; however, the real-life accounts of many people in the educational system served to highlight the messages on the uniqueness of urban schools and the importance of parent involvement to their success.

Finally, it impossible to thank all the individual family members whose personal strength, support, and sacrifice helped us produce this book. Much love and thanks goes to each of you.

Introduction

The challenges of struggling urban schools are among the most troubled and complex aspects of the American educational system. Almost-weekly reports of violence, high dropout rates, demoralized teachers and administrators, teachers' strikes, and substandard academic results have led many observers to claim that urban schools today are the worst of the educational institutions in our nation's history.

Adding to this viewpoint is the belief by some individuals and organizations that nothing can be done to improve this situation.

From strictly a historical perspective, this dismal picture is in sharp contrast to the atmosphere of urban education during the early twentieth century. In 1919, for example, renowned educator Ellwood Cubberly claimed that America's urban schools were the best in the nation and that they had been that way for over a half of a century.

Furthermore, Cubberly noted that the introduction of the "common school" movement resulted in the expansion of economic opportunities, a reduction of the rate of poverty throughout the nation, a decline in criminal activity, and the elimination of class struggle among various ethnic and racial groups. There is little doubt that Cubberly's views were not incorrect, particularly when he went further to compare the nature and status of rural and urban education from the 1920s to the 1940s. So what happened?

Educators, as well as everyday Americans, have debated this question for decades without much consensus or success. The "Coleman Report," a 1966 study titled *Equality of Educational Opportunities*, without question, was at the center of this debate for several decades.

In an enormous and controversial government-supported report, James S. Coleman revealed that African Americans and non–African American children attended separate but equal schools and that the amount of resources allocated to these educational institutions had virtually no impact on the achievement scores and learning gap of the students who attended these educational facilities.

Thus, Coleman concluded that the differences in the scores of African American and European students were more influenced by family income and peer-group dynamics, rather than teachers and the school environment.

Indeed, the Coleman Report had a profound impact on the theories about the nature of America's urban educational system for the rest of the twentieth century as well as into the twenty-first century. For example, so-called Progressive or Revisionist historians claimed that economic conflicts and social forces were at the center of the United States's urban school crisis. Scholars such as Bernard Bailyn, in his book *Education in the Forging of American Society,* claimed that the growth of public education was linked to and influenced by various societal forces.

These forces, he concluded, shaped the history of America's public school system, which "was a complex story, involving changes in the role of the state as well as in the general institutional character of society."

This interpretation remained dominant in the literature of American urban schools throughout the 1970s. However, at the close of the decade, another group of scholars rose in defense of the accomplishments of public education and urban schools, and thus rejected the arguments articulated by the "Progressives" or "Revisionists." A leader in the effort was scholar Diane Ravitch, an "Neo-Consensus" writer who contended that during the 1920s and 1930s, despite the problems within the bureaucratic levels of urban school, and the enormous biases based on issues of class, ethnicity, gender, and race, urban schools did provide an avenue for upward mobility and helped to integrate immigrants, minorities, and women into the mainstream of American society.

From the 1970s to the mid-1980s, arguments of "Progressive/Revisionists" and "Neo-Consensus/Non-Revisionists" scholars remained dominant in the literature on America's urban schools. The key question that these scholars debated was: Why did urban schools serve as a means for upward mobility and inclusion during the 1920s and 1930s but not in the 1960s and 1970s?

To answer this query, education scholars began to examine school curriculum, the objective and role of America's urban schools, and growing dependence on the educational system in the United States to solve most, if not all, social and economic problems. Some scholars also began to reexamine the influence of social forces and the economic construct on the educational process in various regions, states, cities, and towns.

Since the 1980s to today, another group of scholars, known as "Post-Revisionists," have emerged and tried to move beyond the polarization and oppositionist interpretations articulated by many writers in the earlier decades. These scholars have focused their research and studies on the activities of the working classes and urban minorities themselves, along with their relationships with urban schools. Many scholars viewed these groups of people as merely passive victims in the educational process.

More specifically, the studies produced by these scholars have portrayed urban schools as contested institutions in which the working class, civic organizations, and minority groups clash over the direction of pending changes of various educational policies, practices, funding, and curricula.

There is no doubt that our study fits into this current genre of literature on urban schools. More specifically, our analysis claims that the only way one can truly analyze the educational experience of minority groups, especially African Americans, is to place Black American life at the center of the study. Once this approach in taken, a different picture in regard to education in urban America is revealed.

Furthermore, the purpose of this book is to illustrate that the urban school environment for African American students, on one level, is truly unique. On another level, our book prescribes un-unique solutions to the various problems examined here—massive parental involvement. Indeed, many urban schools are failing in connection to its African American population. However, this situation can be changed with the creation of comprehensive parental involvement plans that take into account the various contradictions, struggles, and situations many African American students and parents face almost daily.

The pages that follow address these concepts in eight compact chapters that reinforce the notion that massive parental involvement will transform America's urban schools in connection to its African American population. From this perspective, we offer numerous local, regional, and national recommendations that are based on historical, qualitative, and quantitative research.

ONE

Parental Involvement and School Culture in the Inner City

Recently, a mother with a teenaged son in a local large inner-city school talked about how she was called away from work because her son was about to be suspended for fighting. When she got to the school and sat down with the principal, she found out that some other boys had been teasing her son because he was shy and heavy. This had been going on for months and the mother was incensed that she had never been notified about the issue.

After her son served a five-day suspension and returned to school, the mother made arrangements every few weeks to show up at the school unannounced to see how her son was doing. The mother said that the teachers, especially the one in the classroom where the fight occurred, seemed somewhat uncomfortable when she came to the school. Ultimately the principal met with her and explained that having a parent come into the school like she did was disruptive to the teachers and interfered with the academic environment.

On another day, the principal approached the same mother and told her that from now on she would need to make an appointment a week in advance to come into the school or to take advantage of the specific activities designed to involve the family members such as open houses and holiday programs. In the end, the mother was very upset that her attention to her son's learning experience was not being valued and that she was seen as a troublemaker rather than a helper. Subsequently, she became so disillusioned with the school and overall local educational system that she withdrew her son from the school and homeschooled him.

Contrast this example with another situation where a child was attending a public school in the same district, but in a more affluent com-

1

munity, and got into a fight. His mother went in for a conference with the principal while the child was serving a three-day suspension. When the child was allowed to return from his suspension, the mother made week- ly unannounced trips to the school and was welcomed by the teachers with open arms. Furthermore, the classroom teacher where the fight orig- inated told the mother that she was happy to have so much involvement from a parent because it made her job easier.

This chapter examines this situation within a larger context by analyz- ing the difference in parental involvement based on the topics, class, and geographical location. More specifically, the pages that follow seek to show how urban school environments are unique and thus have a differ- ent learning culture and atmosphere, compared with their suburban counterparts. As a result many nontraditional techniques and models in the area of parental involvement must be used to improve the education experience for the students who attend our nation's various urban schools. This chapter introduces some of these issues.

Indeed, many studies have viewed parent involvement in schools of- ten based on middle-class standards, norms, and expectations in regard to the linkage between students and parents (Cohen 1974; Delpit 1994; Fine 1984; Hacker 1994; Holt 1968; Ravitch 1983, 1985; Ravitch and Vi- novskis 1995). Furthermore, educators and community advocates in a middle-class setting often think they can create a neat little blueprint for parent outreach that can be adapted to any school setting.

Active parents have planned, implemented, and participated in nu- merous local and regional school initiatives based on middle-class norms. They have organized efforts where parents and staff posted flyers around schools to encourage individuals to attend upcoming Parent–Teacher As- sociation (PTA) meetings. They have sent flyers home with each child. In a school of about four hundred students, perhaps fifty to one hundred parents or more would attend a parent meeting in a largely middle-class environment. These types of parent participation would be considered successful. However, most times these efforts are not effective in an ur- ban school setting.

The outreach efforts described previously that would draw large numbers of parents to meetings at schools in middle-class environments are often not as successful in the inner-city schools. In inner-city schools, Parent–Teacher Organization (PTO) and PTA meetings with ten or fewer parents are often considered successful. The same techniques of putting up flyers around the school and sending announcements home with each student are utilized. Yet the same outreach activities often net significant- ly different results. Furthermore, the results are judged differently, de- pending on the type of school.

A parent organization meeting held its monthly meeting at a local public Montessori school in a middle-class neighborhood where about sixty parents attended. It was said to be one of the strongest, most organized, active, and effective parent groups in the local district. The number of parents present and their enthusiasm about creating and executing various fundraising efforts to support the school was impressive.

This enthusiastic group of parents planned new activities and ro capped successful events they had implemented. They sponsored silent auctions, raffles, candy and food sales, and carnival-like events. Their events raised hundreds of dollars that were given to the school to buy new equipment, supplement extracurricular budgets, and fund field trips and other enrichment activities.

The organization's president and several members expressed regret over the "low turnout," of the meeting, citing the weather as the main reason why sixty and not over one hundred parents attended. Although the turnout consisted of a diverse group of parents of various ages and races, with energy and excitement around supporting the school, the participation was considered light.

Earlier that same day, at around 2:30 p.m., an inner-city school on the other side of town held its monthly PTO meeting. This school had about four hundred students, 99 percent of whom were African American and whose families lived below the national poverty level. Present at this meeting were five parents, ten teachers, and the principal. After the meeting, the PTO president, a parent of a child at the school, indicated that she was pleased with the turnout and excited about some of the ideas they discussed, which included selling candy to raise money for library books and field trips, and a special Friday night social event for parents. Given her enthusiasm and hope for improvement, this meeting could be conceived to be as impressive as the one with the larger turnout.

The fact is that there is a world of difference between schools in middle-class neighborhoods, with mostly middle- to upper-income white families, as opposed to schools located in the inner cities, with large numbers of nonwhite children who live far below the "traditional" middle class. Schools in middle- to upper-class neighborhoods may have all of the resources needed to provide a proper education, including books, school supplies, and highly qualified teachers. They may have the necessary support services, such as medical care and remedial academic initiatives in their building. They may have strong, organized parent groups that support their schools. Even if the schools are located in not-so-safe neighborhoods, their parents organize to get adequate police and community support.

A parent at a suburban high school was concerned about a recent school levy failure. As a result, bus service to the school was canceled. In some urban school districts, the cancellation of bus service may have greatly impacted the ability of students to get to school on time or in some cases at all. But in the case of the suburban high school, the mother said all of the parents were more concerned about where the students were going to park, since so many of them either had cars or had access to their parents' cars. The parking space issue seemed somewhat frivolous compared with the challenges of inner-city school children who may not even get to school, or may have to walk much longer distances or get up an hour earlier to get to school.

Schools with large numbers of poor children are often located in the most poverty-stricken, crime-laden, rundown neighborhoods. A school, like any other organization, needs a solid academic support infrastructure to perform optimally. Many inner-city schools do not have the resources they need to even adequately perform their primary objective of educating children. For example, in some large urban school districts, inner-city schools do not have books and teachers make copies from their books for their students every day. One father with a son in an inner-city school in a large Midwestern school district spoke of his frustrations with his son bringing home copies of a few pages in the Algebra II textbook with the homework assignment every day. His son had trouble comprehending the assignments. The father insisted that the teacher give his son a book to take home every evening. Eventually the teacher complied. "I explained to the teacher that my son needed the entire book so he would have the benefit of all the readings and assignments that build on each other," the dad said. His son ended up getting As on the tests while other students struggled to pass.

In another case, some schools in this same district ran out of paper for the copier and did not have money to buy paper. As a result the students had to wait a few days for homework assignments or teachers ran to an office supply store and bought their own paper. However, some frustrated teachers just dictated assignments to students, while others wrote an assignment on the chalkboard for students to copy.

Some inner-city school classes also are taught by inexperienced teachers or by teachers without credentials in the subjects they are teaching. Often, a long-term substitute is no more than a babysitter because he or she is not certified in the content area in which he or she is teaching that day. As school systems struggle with funding issues and eliminate subjects such as home economics, music, art, and physical education, teachers trained in those areas who have not opted for retraining are used as substitutes where they are needed.

For instance, one teacher in a large Midwestern city only substituted in inner-city schools. Working with inner-city school children was her passion. She had an English degree. Once she had a long-term assignment in an eighth grade math class where the students had not had a qualified math teacher for the first three months of the school year. After three months, the school finally acquired a credentialed math teacher. The English teacher was glad the students finally had a math teacher, but regretted not being able to give them a solid foundation in those first three months. She was especially concerned about the eighth graders, most of whom had a fourth- or fifth-grade understanding of math, and were not ready for high school math.

The types of challenges that regularly exist in inner-city schools are not likely to be present in middle- to upper-class or suburban schools where there is a great deal of individual and organized parent involvement. Parents in those schools often organize around issues of academic deficiency and demand change, and usually get change. It is not likely that organized parents will allow a school to have an unqualified math teacher for three months.

This situation is a type of parent involvement that can take on many forms at a school with active parent participation. A number of parents may regularly volunteer in the classrooms or provide needed administrative support to the teacher. Monthly PTA meeting attendance may average up to two hundred attendees. Schools with these types of parent involvement activities usually have highly qualified teachers and books for each student, and never run out of paper or supplies. The many active parents, particularly with a large, organized PTA, have the kind of influence that would not allow for the types of challenges that would hinder the academic success of the children. But in general there are some key factors that make parental involvement a great challenge in most urban schools.

STUDENT MOBILITY

Urban school principals, teachers, and staff are often challenged by the unexpected and unexplained movement of many of their students. Plagued by factors such as the inability to pay rent or housing costs, homelessness, eviction, domestic violence, condemned homes, and so forth, many families are forced to move often, some seemingly monthly. As a result, children end up attending more than one school in a school year. Multiple school changes are certainly not beneficial to the academic success or well-being of the children. Influxes of new students usually present challenges for schools to provide learning and other support services.

One large urban Midwestern school district, for example, went through a period where each school chose its own reading curriculum. Many schools utilized different curricula that required different books and learning techniques. Children moving from school to school could conceivably use a different reading book in each school. For both teachers and children, a change like that could be very frustrating. Children had to get used to a new teacher. They may have had to start over after only a few short weeks with a new textbook and a new learning strategy. Also, teachers struggle with working to get new children caught up while maintaining academic quality with the rest of the class.

Imagine the differences in the challenges faced between a teacher who has to adapt to continuous high student turnover as opposed to a teacher who may get one or two new students in an entire school year. One principal of an inner-city school recalled that some of her classes experienced nearly 50-percent turnover in students per school year.

So often large urban school districts are criticized for lagging behind suburban schools in student academic performance. Student mobility makes academic performance difficult for the student and emphasis on school involvement for the parent nearly impossible. A mother regretted moving her three children several times over a two-year period. She admitted that all three children, ages seven, nine, and twelve, were at least a grade level behind, and at some point had not attended school for months. She also admitted that her focus had been on finding shelter and food for her family, and not on parent involvement activities in the school.

One principal related that he had just enrolled a family of five children, in second through eighth grade, whose children had not been in school in over a year. None of the children were immediately ready to perform academically at their designated grade level. As a result, the principal and some of the teachers discussed possible intervention strategies, such as acquiring tutors and mentors for the new students. The principal was even more concerned because the children appeared to have severe learning disabilities and thus questioned whether or not the school would be able to accommodate their special needs.

Children whose families move frequently also may have to go through a difficult process to make new friends. Or they may be missing old friends. Some children also may not make friends at all. Peer interaction between children can be challenging in normal circumstances. Situations where families move a great deal must be traumatic for children who have to deal with change in a way that many children in other academic settings may not experience.

Frequently local social service agencies house homeless families and help them transition into permanent housing. These agencies have an understanding with the principal of the nearest neighborhood school that the school would accept homeless children housed at the agencies that were usually transferring from different schools. The principal said that some of the children she saw were second grade aged and beyond, and had never been in school.

The principal described the challenges associated with trying to teach a second grade student, who is seven or eight years old, to read when many of their classmates have already developed some basic reading skills. She also talked about the stigma that the homeless child feels being behind the rest of the class. This often plays itself out in behavioral problems brought on by the frustration of having to suffer through the teasing by classmates or just the embarrassment of not knowing how to read. She described incidences of homeless children fighting, talking back to teachers, skipping classes, and just being generally disruptive in classes.

Some principals expressed their frustrations having to put some children in classrooms one to two grades below their actual grade level. Several local inner-city schools have many over-aged children in classes with children two to three years younger than themselves. School officials often describe children in classes with students much younger than they are as disruptive, often having discipline problems, which may likely be caused by a lack of self-esteem about their current situation. Other children in these situations were characterized as withdrawn or uninterested in school.

Mobility also has an impact on areas outside the classroom. A school nurse told me that LensCrafters offered free vision screening to all students in the second month of the school year. The screening occurred over a three-day period. She noted that in those three days, twelve new students enrolled in the school. Those twelve students, not initially anticipated by the nurse, received the vision screenings.

The nurse also expressed concerns about how mobility affected scoliosis screenings. She was required to test sixth through eighth grade students for scoliosis, a spinal condition. According to the nurse, scoliosis should be resolved before a child reaches puberty and bone growth has completed to prevent serious back problems later in life. The nurse tested children at her school in the third grade because so many children were one or more grades behind because they had moved and changed schools many times. Parents of students with potential problems identified in the screening are advised by the nurse to take their children to a doctor for further examination. In comparison, those parents who do not have access to such doctors are left to fend for themselves in the complex and sometimes confusing healthcare system of today.

UNQUALIFIED TEACHERS

It seems ironic that schools with the most academically deficient students, with the most special needs children, as well as the most behaviorally challenged students, often get the teachers least equipped to help them succeed. In *The Shame of the Nation* (2005), Jonathon Kozol describes his visits to schools with unqualified teachers. In one middle school in Harlem, thirteen of fifteen teachers were "provisionals," which meant they were not fully certified to teach. Kozol describes a school in urban Oklahoma City where teachers averaged less than five years experience; teachers elsewhere in the district averaged twelve years. He mentions other situations where teachers worked under "emergency credentials," meaning that they are not yet certified to teach the subject they are teaching, but the school had a vacancy that needed to be filled.

The percentage of classes taught by teachers who do not have a major in the subject they are teaching is far greater in high-poverty, high-minority schools than in low-poverty, low-minority schools (Kunjufu 2002). "A North Carolina study estimates that 25% of inner city school teachers are unqualified to teach the subjects they are assigned to instruct." A 2005 National Center for Education Statistics (NCES) report on mobility in the teacher workforce indicated that in general, new hires are more likely to be younger and to teach out of field than continuing teachers. A 2010 report by the Education Trust indicated that core academic classes in high-poverty secondary schools are almost twice as likely to have an out-of-field teacher as counterpart classes in low-poverty schools (Almy and Theokas 2010).

Mobility among new teachers in inner-city schools is troubling. At least 40 percent of inner-city school teachers transfer within five years (Kunjufu 2002). One teacher spent about four years teaching in a tough inner-city school in a large New England city. She taught fourth grade language arts. She said that she spent most of her class time breaking up fights, telling students to be quiet, and getting "talked back to" by children who should have been fifth or sixth graders.

The teacher was frustrated with her inability to connect with parents. Most of the parents of the children did not return her phone calls or notes sent home with the student, and as she recalled, fewer than ten parents in four years ever showed up for a parent–teacher conference. She recalled being so excited when she graduated from college and was going to a poor, black middle school to "make a difference." After four frustrating years, she resigned from her teaching position and took a job as a management trainee at a bank.

Some inner-city schools have teachers who have been in these schools for many years, and have been ineffective for one reason or another. Some are apathetic. Some are "burned out" over the constant challenges. Some teach just for the money. Some may just need more professional development. The vast majorities of the teachers are competent and hardworking, and want to help children succeed. Only a portion fit into the category of ineffectiveness. But even one is too many.

Some schools have more than their share of long-term substitutes. Teachers may or may not be certified or experienced in subjects that they are teaching. Teachers who are long-term substitutes without knowledge of their areas of instruction can do a great disservice to children by keeping them academically deficient and not ready to advance to the next grade level.

Even short-term substitute teachers who are properly credentialed face challenges. One substitute teacher in a large Southern school district taught for a few days in a science class. She was formerly a certified science teacher who left full-time teaching to spend more time with her children. The principal was glad to get a credentialed science teacher for those few days. The teacher regretted that she could only spend a few days with a class that had such a strong need for a science teacher, as her intent was only to fill a temporary need; yet the permanent teacher was expected to be out for several weeks.

RACE AND RACISM

Race, racism, and its various permutations have been studied intensely by a plethora of scholars over the past few decades. For instance, in a recent study Richard Thompson Ford, the George E. Osborne Professor of Law at Stanford School of Law, noted that there is a clear difference between "overt" racism and "institutional" racism. More specifically, in our public schools institutional racism can manifest itself in a variety of ways, such as in low expectations and low test scores for a certain segment of the student population, the attitudes of unqualified teachers, the ability to track the academic abilities of some pupils, and the use of a range of discipline methods.

From a historical perspective, some scholars have argued that institutional racism has been embedded in America's public educational system since its inception to maintain the lower socioeconomic status of certain racial and ethnic groups and eventually exploit them as laborers. In his seminal work, *The American School, 1642–1993* (1994), Joel Spring states, "segregation in public schools in the United States was directly related to maintaining an inexpensive source of labor" (162). When legal segregation ended, various ethnic groups began to demand "that public schools recognize their distinct cultures and incorporate these cultures into the curricula and textbooks" (185). Spring concluded that in the end, however, this situation has led many people, especially people of color, to question "how the control of knowledge can be used as an instrument of power" (216).

This claim is echoed further in another study by Jaleel K. Abdul-Adil and Alvin David Farmer, Jr. (2006), who claim that despite being treated differently, parental involvement for African Americans in urban schools will increase if three concepts are enhanced: (1) empowerment, (2) outreach, and (3) indigenous resources. Such strategies, Abdul-Adil and Farmer, Jr., conclude, will not only increase parental involvement in the overall function of the school but also lead to better educational success for the students themselves (Abdul-Adil and Farmer 2006).

POVERTY

Poverty is a prevalent characteristic of inner-city schools. In many urban school districts, a large percentage of children qualify for free or reduced lunch, which means they come from families living at or below the national poverty level.

The kinds of contributions parents can make to school success vary greatly among schools. Parents in a local public school in an affluent neighborhood donated money for extra computers and supplies. At a similar school, parents contributed the money to help the school build a small kitchenette on the first floor to support school events in the auditorium, which was also on the first floor. The cafeteria was located on the lower level, and was inconvenient when the school sponsored events in the auditorium.

Jonathon Kozol (2005) describes a school in Manhattan that raised nearly $50,000 per year to hire a writing teacher and two part-time music teachers. Parents raising children in poverty cannot necessarily contribute financially to the benefit of the schools. Most are concerned about providing food, clothing, and housing for their families.

Poverty is not just a recent phenomenon that has impacted urban public education. This issue has plagued America's urban educational system for many decades. More specifically, the topic of school funding has been a hotly debated topic for many scholars, policy makers, politicians, administrators, and teachers probably since the 1966 study, *Equality of Educational Opportunity*, better known as the "Coleman Report," was published.

In this massive study, Coleman found that in terms of available resources, African American and White children essentially attended separate but equal educational facilities and the level of economic resources that were allocated to such schools had little to no impact on the academic achievement of the students. Coleman further noted that families and peer groups played a more significant role on the academic success of students than did teachers or the school environment. Thus, since the mid-1960s, these claims have shaped every discussion in regard to poverty and school funding in connection to urban education in our nation.

CRIME AND VIOLENCE

Young Americans have been killing one another in unprecedented numbers during the past few decades. Newspaper articles, television reports, and websites have been barraged with daily reports of various tragedies of young men and women whose lives have been crippled or completely destroyed by violence. Killings on school campuses have impacted communities all over the country. Such incidents at the campus of Columbine High School (Colorado) in 1999, Dunbar High School (Illinois) in 2009, and most recently Sandy Hook School (Connecticut) in 2012 are just a few of the most recent, horrific examples.

Inner-city school administrators have to deal more often than not with the possibility of crime and violence within or in the vicinity of the school. One large Midwestern city urban school principal described the common occurrence of having to confiscate knives and guns from children in her elementary school! She even sent kindergartners home for bringing weapons to school.

Another elementary school principal described how once all the staff and children laid on the ground while drug dealers across the street engaged in a shootout. Another principal described the day the police led a female eighth grade student away from the school in handcuffs because she had seriously injured another child in a fight on the playground.

A shooting that involved several teens occurred in the parking lot of a restaurant across the street from one inner-city high schools. Two boys were shot and one sustained serious injuries. Although the shooting occurred off school grounds, the close proximity of the restaurant to the school prompted the media to associate the incident with the school.

Many parents are very concerned about the crime and violence in the vicinity of schools. Often parents who have the opportunity or means to send their children to schools outside the inner city will do so, citing crime and violence in the neighborhood as a concern.

At PTO meetings at a school in a large Midwestern city, one single mother of a second grader who lived a block from the school constantly complained of gunfire heard sporadically in the area throughout the day and more regularly in the evening. She walked her daughter to and from school every day and was fearful that eventually they would fall victim to stray bullets or some criminal activity. When her daughter reached the fourth grade, they moved to a quiet suburban community outside of the large Midwestern city where they had previously lived.

HEALTH AND WELLNESS

In many major cities, large numbers of children suffer from potentially disabling and fatal illnesses. School-aged children in the United States miss nearly fifteen million school days yearly due to asthma alone (Forbis et al. 2006). And others have diabetes and other illnesses that require medical attention. Often urban schools do not have a nurse on staff, or the nurse may be on duty only a day or two per week. Children with health problems often have to leave school to go to the hospital or to see a doctor.

Some large urban school districts have partnered with health clinics to provide services at schools on specified days during the week, and some schools even have a health clinic built into the school that is open to the community as well as students. The Promise Academy Charter Schools in New York, founded by Geoffrey Canada in a partnership with the Harlem Children's Zone, Inc., has a health clinic in the middle school. Students receive free medical, dental, and mental health services as needed during the school day. Such a set-up in the school provides a great service to children and to their parents.

An unresolved health condition can cause a student to miss a lot of school, or to be ineffective in school. One teacher recalled a student in her inner-city fifth grade class who was always participative and engaging. Lately he had become withdrawn, combative with some of his friends, and just plain uncooperative. She finally spoke with the mother of the boy who admitted that she had lost her job and had no money to pay for her son to visit a dentist for a severe toothache. The teacher was able to refer the mother to a free clinic where the boy was given the dental attention that he needed, and his behavior went back to normal when he no longer had to endure the intense pain of a toothache.

An example of an inner-city school with unique challenges is Roosevelt High School. Roosevelt (not its real name) is representative of many schools in inner-city environments. It is located in a low-income neighborhood, with the majority of the children living in poverty. The school has many issues that schools in middle- to upper-class settings may not have.

Roosevelt High School is located in the inner core of a large Midwestern city. It is part of the city school district, which consists of about thirty-five thousand students. Nearly 71 percent of the district's students are African American, 24 percent are White, and the other 5 percent are of other races or are multinational. About 66 percent of the students qualify for free or reduced rate lunch, meaning they are living in families with total incomes at or below the national poverty level.

Roosevelt is located in the poorest neighborhood in the city. The average annual family income in this community is less than 10,000 dollars. Roosevelt is housed in an historic ninety-thousand-square-foot structure built in the early 1900s. Though Roosevelt is a uniquely beautiful architectural structure, the school is surrounded by dilapidated apartment buildings and a vacant lot, along with some factories and empty buildings. The buildings are very close together and virtually no green space exists in the vicinity of the school.

Several young men, mostly young African Americans, were always standing on the street corners opposite the school. Most of these males appeared to be teenagers or young adults in their early to middle twenties. These individuals were drug dealers. It is hard to believe that these young men were spending the better part of their days selling drugs on the street. Teachers, students, and parents knew they were drug dealers.

At any given time of the day or night, these young men would approach cars, from the worst beat up vehicles to the high-priced fancy models, and hand the driver a package, and appear to receive a large wad of money. These drug deals would take place often in broad daylight, in close proximity to the school. Any student looking out of a classroom window or standing on the playground became a witness to a crime.

Many shootings took place in the neighborhood surrounding Roosevelt. Some have happened within a few blocks of the school. Most people believe the shootings are drug related. A parent said that she knew a man who was shot and killed near the school. She said he was shot in a dispute over payment for drugs. She said those kinds of disputes were common in that neighborhood. This hardly sounds like an appropriate environment for a school.

However, open crime and violence is a way of life for many inner-city residents. Some parents and students talk about hearing what sounds like gun shots everyday at various times of the day. Students at Roosevelt talked about witnessing criminal activity, such as theft and prostitution, from the windows of the school building.

One administrator in an inner-city school described a spring afternoon where school let out at 2:30 p.m. Students, teachers, staff, and administrators were greeted at the entrance to the building by gunfire. Allegedly, some drug dealers were fighting over "turf," or at least that was the speculation of that administrator. He recalled everyone, children and adults alike, hitting the ground and or diving for cover. What a harrowing experience for a school full of innocent children and adults!

At any given time, the drug dealers lingered around the school, sometimes within the fenced-in playground of the school after school hours. This is not a book about the ills and evils of drug dealing. The intent here is to show a clear distinction between that particular inner-city school environment and many residential and suburban school settings.

The school principal at Roosevelt had over thirty years experience in teaching and administration at inner-city schools in Southern urban cities before he came to Roosevelt. He was retired at the time and planned to pursue college teaching. He was eager to share his success with college students and enjoy his retirement from inner-city school teaching and administration.

However, he was lured back into school administration by the local superintendent, who was familiar with his successes as a principal. Possessing a reputation as a results-getter in tough urban school settings, he was heavily recruited by the school superintendent to take over what was described to him as "the worst school in the district." He remembered thinking that he wanted to take one more shot at making a difference in the lives of children, so he decided to come out of his retirement to take on the challenges of Roosevelt.

When the new principal arrived at Roosevelt in 2001, the building was in poor condition. The principal recalled counting one hundred broken windows. Graffiti lined the inside walls throughout the building. Litter, including broken glass, was sprawled around the outside of the building. A steel fence surrounding the playground was jagged and presented a safety hazard. Drug dealers frequented the playground and parking lot of the school at any given time, even during school hours.

The principal immediately took on the task of cleaning up the physical structure. He had all the windows repaired. He secured a donation of paint from a local hardware store, and staff and volunteers painted all the walls in the school. He insisted that the plant manager keep the inside and outside grounds litter-free, and he constantly inspected the grounds for litter. He contacted local officials about the jagged fence and persisted until the city sent someone out to replace it.

He also appealed to the drug dealers that frequented the grounds by befriending them. He talked to them about sports and music, and as they got more comfortable with him, he described to them his vision for a better school for the children, and asked them to stay clear of the grounds, but to keep watch over the children. The drug dealers agreed not to come onto school grounds, and to stay across the street from the school. They truly accepted their role as protectors of the students, as well as the school.

One day, one of the known drug dealers came into the building to warn the principal that the police were ticketing teachers' cars. The staff parking lot was being resurfaced, so several employees parked on the street in no-parking zones. By the time the principal got outside to try to appeal to the police officer, he was gone and no cars had been ticketed. The drug dealer explained to him that he showed the police officer that the parking lot was being resurfaced and convinced him that the cars should not be ticketed, and the officer agreed and left.

Before the new principal's tenure, Roosevelt had a reputation for being a school riddled with disciplinary issues. Students roamed the hallways at all hours. Cursing and fighting were present at all grade levels, including the preschool. School staff regretted that they could not put posters or student artwork on the walls because students would defame them or tear them down.

Under the new leadership, students were taught to speak to adults and their peers respectfully and to respect school property. One parent with a fourth grader remarked that finally he could walk throw the halls without getting hit by a wad of paper or pushed out of the way or cursed at by a student. Another parent commented that the new principal's first year was the first time in many years that the school was able to put up a Christmas tree without students pulling it down!

Students no longer roamed the halls during school hours. They were usually present in the halls only during passing of classes, lunchtime, or under extreme circumstances. Fighting among students became the exception, and not the rule.

The principal started the policy that all students wear uniforms to school, which further demonstrated the commitment to a more disciplined, structured learning environment. Initially, that rule was not readily enforced, as the principal did not want to encourage children to stay home because they could not afford uniforms. Ultimately, they relaxed the policy by requiring children to wear a white top and black, blue, or khaki bottoms to school. That was helpful to the parents as well, who did not have to go out shopping for new clothes.

Inner-city schools often have large numbers of special-needs children, many with severe learning disabilities, creating additional challenges for teaching staff. One local school district reported that about 18 percent of its students are special needs, although a number of the schools in the inner city exceed that figure by as much as 10 to 15 percent. One inner-city high school principal in a large Midwestern city estimated that over one third of his students had some sort of learning disability.

More specifically, a particular student at Roosevelt had a condition that rendered him unable to sit in a classroom for long periods. He was an attractive, intelligent young man, but became increasingly disinterested and irritated with the traditional classroom surroundings after a short time. One day he caused a huge commotion among the staff and students when he disrupted a music class by throwing books, instruments, and whatever he could get his hands on around the classroom. His mother was concerned he would be expelled from school.

As an alternative to expulsion, his mother, the principal, and his teachers worked together to develop an individualized education plan (IEP) for the student. This plan sought to organize and arrange strategies and activities designed to help a special-needs child excel in school. His IEP required that after a specified period, and whenever he became agitated, he would spend time in a separate room, usually the parent center, supervised by a staff member, until he was calm enough to go back to class. Imagine the institutional and logistical challenges of a school with large numbers of special-needs students, all with different specifications on how their educational experience is to be handled!

The principal entered Roosevelt in its second year of what the state calls *school redesign*. Redesign is part of a five-year school improvement plan mandated by the state Department of Education for all public schools not meeting academic success as indicated by standardized tests. As part of the redesign, all existing staff were released and had to reapply for their jobs.

The new principal decided that to change the environment, he had to get rid of teachers he thought were enabling failure. After extensive interviews and contemplation, the principal elected to retain one teacher from the previous staff. The new teaching staff averaged six years of teaching experience, substantially less than the district's average of twelve years. However, he preferred this more inexperienced staff to the former, where over half were essentially functioning long-term substitutes, many of who were not certified in the subject areas in which they were teaching.

At a school board meeting prior to the new principal's tenure, a small group of teachers, community advocates, and parents from Roosevelt spoke during a special segment of the meeting where members of the public were free to speak to the board on topics of interest to them. In the allotted three minutes, they described how Roosevelt was producing classes of students that had progressed through three grades without certified permanent teachers. They expressed the dismay that these children were being passed to the next grade level without demonstrating proficiency in the current level, and that the oldest children were going to high school academically unprepared.

That this sort of situation could be allowed to take place is disturbing. Imagine students going into high school without the benefit of having learned the basics! How does a high school child, at a time when peer interaction and appearance is so important, who is reading at a fourth grade level ever catch up to his or her peers? Those students who have the courage to admit they have problems may get the remedial help they need to succeed. The rest may drop out of school.

The principal felt that the staff he had assembled was an effective mixture of inexperienced and experienced teachers. Though many teachers were relatively new to the profession, many who had between ten and twenty years of experience in other schools came to Roosevelt under the new principal. He agreed that many teachers still needed significant teaching experience and professional development geared toward working in culturally diverse and inner-city school environments. He was convinced, however, that they had the potential to become one of the most successful teaching staffs in the district.

PRINCIPAL AS COUNSELOR TO BOTH PARENTS AND STUDENTS

Inner-city school principals often have to be more than just administrators. The Roosevelt principal said, "Here, you have to deal with the non-academic issues; you have to be a father figure, you have to work outside the box of a principal."

He fondly recalled several instances where he felt more like a counselor than a principal: "Fathers and grandfathers come in to talk to me. I have had conversations with fathers recently released from jail—I've encouraged them to be involved with their children and their [children's] education. I talk to parents and they will tell me things, then thank me for taking the time to listen to them."

Sometimes parents of children who do not get along end up having disagreements themselves over their children. Parents care about their children and will naturally defend their honor. The principal invited two mothers whose sons fought all the time to the school to discuss the situation concerning the boys. By the time he went out into the hall to greet the two ladies and invite them into his office, they were yelling at each other. He remembered telling them, "Don't come in here ranting and raving or I'll have both of you locked up!" That statement got the attention of both women, and after they calmed down, the principal took them into his office and told each one of them her son was bad. They all laughed and talked the situation out and the ladies left on good terms.

The principal admitted that because Roosevelt is a neighborhood school and many of the parents know each other, he sometimes inadvertently got in the middle of disputes between parents or families. He recalled a situation where two mothers came into to talk to him about their children not getting along, but when he had the ladies in his office he found out that they had recently argued in a venue outside the school. He recalled saying to them, "That's not why we're here, but since you brought it up, let's get it out and resolve it!" He successfully led the ladies to a resolution about their personal conflicts, and then they were able to talk about their children's situation.

Often the principal mediated situations between mothers and fathers regarding their child where there was obviously discord between the parents, one of which was often noncustodial. Roosevelt also had a number of students living in foster care situations. Sometimes the principal found himself in the middle of disputes between foster parents and natural parents over issues regarding a child's performance or behavior.

The principal believed that Roosevelt's challenges could be improved through greater parental involvement, so he set out to create a more friendly school environment. He said his ideal picture of parent involvement was "parent volunteers in the classroom and parent center." He converted an empty classroom into a parent center. The parent center had adult-sized tables and chairs, a couch, computer, microwave, refrigerator, sink, and telephone. Parents could always come to the parent center in the morning and get a hot cup of coffee and a donut.

The new principal was an experienced administrator who understood the challenges of the inner-city school environment. He was convinced that active parent involvement at the parent center, in the classrooms, and in the PTO would give parents the confidence to advocate for the best conditions for their children and for the school.

A CHARTER SCHOOL IN THE INNER CITY

Indigo Academy (not its real name) is a charter school located in the inner city of a large Midwestern city. The school houses six hundred children in grades prekindergarten through eight. About 98 percent of the children are African American; 2 percent are of other races. Indigo was started about eight years ago and is owned by a corporation that runs charter schools throughout the Midwest. About 60 percent of the teachers

are African American; the rest are White. Indigo occupies a former traditional school building and is located in a low-income community with
high crime.

The school director is the primary administrator. She reports to a principal who splits her time between Indigo and another school campus in a
different city. Therefore, the director has responsibility for day-to-day
operations of the school.

She finds herself having to be ready to talk to parents at any time.
"You have to be able to counsel the children and counsel the parents,"
she said. Many Indigo parents never finished high school, or started and
never finished college. She believes that the more the parents better themselves, the better supporters they are of their children. "I have had two
parents that I convinced to go back to college, and their children are
doing so much better because their mothers are moving forward."

The director encouraged one parent who worked in the lunchroom to
go back to school. The parent obtained a GED and an associate's degree
and is now working at a hospital making twice the income she made at
the school. And her two children are among the best students in their
respective classes.

She admits that not all parents appreciate her strong counseling. "Not
every parent feels the need to move to a different level. I can't tell you
how many times I've been cussed or told to mind my own business." But
still she perseveres. "Some parents are listening and want direction, and
we try to provide that for them."

REFLECTIONS

Because inner-city school have a different and sometimes unique culture,
educators and administrators must be flexible in what is a potentially
dynamic and disruptive environment. They must be willing to contest
traditional modes of operation to overcome unique challenges and provide successful educational experience for students.

TWO

Why Bother with Engaging Parents?

Why bother going through all of the trouble to engage parents, particularly in those circumstances when parents are not already active? Why do we need parents involved in schools and in their children's education? Why put educators through the time, cost, frustration, and energy of trying to recruit parents and keep them actively engaged in the educational process? The answer is that parental involvement will enable parents to help schools become more effective educational facilities and in the long run benefit all children. This chapter seeks to examine this claim in some detail.

PARENT INVOLVEMENT AND ACADEMIC ACHIEVEMENT

Today it is widely accepted that parental involvement is directly linked to higher academic achievement. For example, in Angela C. Baum and Paula McMurray-Schwarz's article "Preservice Teachers' Beliefs about Family Involvement" (2004), the authors claim that students whose parents are involved in their education exhibit more positive signs toward school and homework, in comparison with their cohorts whose lack such family involvement.

Gail L. Thompson also echoes this sentiment when she argues that "it is well known that parental involvement is positively correlated to academic achievement" (2003, 8). Furthermore, she contends that parental involvement for urban and lower socioeconomic labeled schools can be enhanced by "connecting with parents/guardians in ways that make them feel welcome and valued." Current research further shows that many school choice or charter school programs directly rest upon a high level of parental involvement. For example, in 2000 educational consultant Philip Vassallo conducted a detailed study on school choice programs in Milwaukee, Wisconsin, San Antonio, Texas, and Dayton, Ohio. His analysis revealed that parents of students in school choice and charter school institutions tended to be more engaged in their child's academic endeavors, participated in more school-sponsored activities, and believed that their schools offered a greater measure of safety, discipline, and quality of instruction, compared with their previous educational facility.

Furthermore, Vassallo's study (2000) uncovered various statistics about school choice and charter school programs on the city, state, and national levels that suggest that charter school programs "support parents' involvement in their children's studies, encourage parents' participation in meaningful school activities, [and] engender greater satisfaction" (13–14) by all involved parties.

Belinda is a parent whose three children attend a public charter school in a large Midwestern city that has a nationally recognized record of academic success. All her children are performing well academically. She attributes a significant part of their success to the school opening its doors to parents like her, who never finished high school. "Even though I dropped out myself, they still welcome me in the building and value my help in the classroom and volunteering on projects," Belinda said.

Scott F. Abernathy's 2004 study reveals similar claims in a short but potent piece titled "Charter Schools, Parents, and Public Schools in Minnesota." In this analysis, the author claims that most successful low-income charter schools view parental involvement as not only useful but essential to the policies and activities of the school. More specifically, Abernathy contends that "parental involvement is considered most useful in those areas of school policy that more directly affect standards toward which students should aspire, the curriculum that serves to get them there, and the discipline policy" (5) of the educational facility.

Indeed, parents are the life support system of children. The most important support a child can receive comes from the home. Parents sustain their children's learning when they ensure that students arrive at school rested, fed, and ready to learn, as well as when they set high learning expectations and nurture their children's self-esteem (White 1998).

Most school administrators, teachers, parents, and even students believe in the principle that the involvement of parents will improve the academic performance of children as well as increase the value of the schooling process overall. A child whose parents ask about his or her homework is more likely to get it done, even if the parent does not understand the assignments.

Some parents at Roosevelt knew that their children were struggling academically and arranged tutors for them. Furthermore, many of the teachers who had good relationships with parents alerted them to the problems that their children were having in school and worked with them to find solutions through free tutoring programs, specialists assigned to the school, or other community resources.

In a survey of 11,317 parents of children in forty-one schools in a large suburban school district located in a metropolitan area, James Griffith (1996) concluded that there is a direct correlation between parent involvement and higher standardized test scores. Schools that had higher levels of parent involvement had higher student test scores. Parent involvement activities on the survey included participating in volunteer activities at the school, attending Parent–Teacher Association (PTA) meetings, and being present at school activities such as open houses, as well as participating in various school governance events.

Some researchers also have illustrated how students' attitudes and behaviors work as processes that promote achievement as well as how home, school, and church support directly affect these processes. For example, a study (Sanders 1988) of 827 African American eighth-grade students was conducted in a school district in a southeastern city, with a population of approximately three hundred thousand and a student body of about forty-two thousand. Students completed surveys that asked questions that covered the following topics: (1) teacher support, (2) parental support, (3) church involvement, (4) achievement ideology, (5) academic self-concept, (6) school behavior, and (7) academic achievement (self-reported grades in social studies, science, English, and mathematics). The results of the study suggested "that providing encouragement and guidance, significant adults in the family, church, and school help students to develop the attitudes and behaviors necessary for school success" (Sanders 1998, 401).

Parents also can have a significant impact on the classroom performance of children. One teacher discussed increased mathematics aptitude among the student population of her second-grade class of inner-city students when she designed a program that involved parents in helping their children learn basic math concepts, such as time and money. Her class contained twenty-two students, all but one living below the poverty level. Thirteen students were classified as (English as a second language learners. She sent packets home with the students that parents were to work on with their children. A pretest showed that 50 percent of the students mastered the concepts and a posttest indicated 77 percent achieved mastery (Carey 1998).

Furthermore, Nancy Hill and Stacie Craft (2003) indicated that African American parents' presence in the classroom may provide them with information about the skills required by the teacher and enhance their ability to promote and develop these skills in their children. They interviewed 103 kindergarten parents and their children randomly from three ethnically diverse elementary schools from a public school system in a southeastern semiurban city.

The parents represented all income and education levels. Parents were interviewed about their involvement in their child's education and children's abilities to navigate social situations were assessed. Hill and Craft finally concluded that parents' involvement at school, including volunteering in the classroom and sending materials to school, improved children's academic skills, which in turn improved math performance for African American children.

Frederick Hampton, Dawne Mumford, and Lloyd Bond (1998) described the Project FAST (Families Are Students and Teachers) program conducted in five kindergarten classrooms in East Cleveland, Ohio, between 1993 and 1996. This community is 99 percent African American, 69 percent from single-parent households, and 49 percent from families living below the poverty level.

Project FAST included monthly parent workshops teaching parents to reinforce instruction at home and help create a home environment that fosters learning. The program required that teachers communicate regularly with parents. Although actual statistics were not provided, the authors claimed that student achievement in reading, language arts, and mathematics in four of the five classrooms rose significantly above that of students not participating in the program.

Another study (Marcon 1999) looked at seven hundred African American preschoolers in Washington, D.C., that used teacher reports of parent involvement. The researcher compared students' grades and skill ratings. Parents with high involvement ratings, compared with those with low or median ratings, tended to have children with higher grades and scores. This finding held across all family income levels and backgrounds (Marcon 1999).

In their retrospective study, Wendy Miedel and Arthur Reynolds (1999) analyzed interviews from seven hundred parents of eighth graders in Chicago. In addition to their background and expectations for their children, parents reported on their involvement when their children were in preschool and kindergarten. Seventy percent had been engaged in Chicago Parent Centers, which offered workshops and information about children's learning, as well as activities to help parents be involved at school. To confirm parents' reports, teachers rated parents' participation in school activities. These teacher ratings closely matched what the parents said.

Miedel and Reynolds (1999) compared results for students based on how much their parents had been involved. Between first and eighth grades, students whose parents took part in a greater number of activities at the school tended to earn higher scores on reading tests, spend less time in special education, and pass from one grade to the next. These findings held across all family backgrounds.

Looking at low-income African American students from sixty-two families during the transition between fifth and sixth grades, Leslie Gutman and Carol Midgley (2000) asked what helped them through the change. They found that the combined effect of parent and school support had a significant impact on middle school grades. Students reported on three key influences:

- Parent involvement: talking to students about school, checking homework, attending events, and volunteering at school
- Support from teachers: taking time to help students and being supportive rather than critical
- Belonging at school: feeling accepted, respected, and included at school

Relating these factors to grade point averages, the researchers found that no single factor appeared to have an effect. When the researchers combined parent involvement with the other two factors, however, another picture emerged. Students reporting high parent involvement and a high sense of belonging, or high parent involvement and high teacher support, had higher grades than students who reported low support at home and school.

Joyce Epstein (2001) discovered in a survey of parents of over 1,269 Maryland school children that despite generally positive attitudes, parents believed that the schools could do more to involve them In learning activities to help their children at home. Epstein noted that surprisingly large numbers of parents were excluded from some of the most basic, traditional communications from the school, such as specific memos, conversations, phone calls, or conferences with teachers about their child's progress or problems in school.

Epstein has identified six types of parent involvement that are widely accepted in the field of education. The six items are (1) open communication between school and parents, (2) parent roles supported, (3) connection with student learning, (4) volunteers welcome, (5) partners in school decisions, and (6) community involvement.

Forrest Benson and Sean Martin's article "Organizing Successful Parental Involvement in Urban Schools" reveals some similar notions. In this brief but potent study, Benson and Martin explore the successful parental involvement strategies that were employed in several public schools in Buffalo, New York. The authors contend that when teachers take coherent and deliberate action to involve parents from minority-based or lower-socioeconomic-status schools, the level of parental participation will increase dramatically.

Benson and Martin suggest that the following steps must be instituted: (1) "focus on student's success and achievements"; (2) send "personalized invitations to parent and child"; (3) work with available "extended family" members; (4) create several useful school staff and volunteer networks; and (5) develop a coordinated plan between administrators, teachers, parents, and students (189). Such goals can be structured as parent volunteer programs, award assemblies, or parent–teacher workshops.

Abe Feuerstein's study (2000) showed similar findings from his research of parent involvement in over one thousand schools. Feuerstein indicated that researchers must "investigate how to help school leaders identify practices and policies that encourage parent trust and involvement in the process of schooling " (38). He selected a nationally representative sample of 1,052 schools, focusing on 24,599 eighth graders and their families. His research was based on questionnaires completed by the students, their parents, and their principals. The research suggested that parent involvement could increase with outreach to parents by teachers.

Administrators and advocates may need to explore parent involvement initiatives that are different from the traditional activities schools engaged in currently. Laura Desimone (1999) studied surveys from approximately twenty-one thousand parents of eighth grade students in the National Education Longitudinal Study of 1988, which included survey data and standardized test scores for a randomly sampled, nationally representative group. Desimone's research suggests that the effectiveness of particular parent involvement practices differ according to race, ethnicity, and family income.

Desimone concludes that more study needs to be done to determine what types of parent involvement are effective for diverse groups of people. For example, for low-income students, Parent–Teacher Organization (PTO) involvement was nonsignificant for all types of achievement, and for middle-income students, it predicted an increase in mathematics and reading. Interestingly enough, PTO involvement seemed to be a better indicator for the academic success of African American students than students of any other racial or ethnic group.

Parent involvement is important for student expectations and in monitoring student behavior. According to a study of 1,200 New England urban students, when parents actively participate in their child's school and interact with their child's teacher, they gain a greater understanding of the expectations that schools have for students and learn how they can enhance their own child's learning at home (Izzo, Weissberg, Kasprow, and Fendrich 1999).

Parents who take the time to find out what is going on in their child's school, who monitor homework assignments, and who show up for conferences when asked are far more likely to wind up with disciplined, responsible youngsters than those who do not stay involved (Lazares 1999). One eighth grade student at Roosevelt admitted that although she knew her mother did not understand her homework, she was always encouraged that she asked to see it and kept track of when it was due. Her mother was a high school dropout who could barely read. This student was first in her class.

PARENT INVOLVEMENT AND THE GOVERNMENT

Should the government be involved in fostering parent involvement in education? There are those who argue that the government should stay out of just about everything. However, the government has been involved in education since very early in U.S. history. But what value does the government place on parent involvement in education? Great value, apparently. Education legislation aimed at improving the performance of the nation's schools includes support for parent involvement.

In 1965, as part of the "War on Poverty," a federal initiative under President Lyndon B. Johnson designed to improve the plight of the poor, Congress passed the Elementary and Secondary Education Act (ESEA). ESEA is a government initiative created to provide children from low-income families with the adequate resources necessary to succeed in school. Title I of the ESEA provides funds for textbooks and other instructional materials and services in public schools.

Title I funding is allocated to schools that have a majority of students whose families live at or below the national poverty level, or who qualified for free or reduced-cost lunch. As a requirement for receipt of Title I funding, school districts must earmark at least 1 percent of the funds for parent-involvement programs (Kessler-Sklar and Baker 2000).

The guidelines are somewhat vague on exactly how Title I money should be spent. Funds are spent on parenting workshops, presentations, and even some social gatherings at the school. Schools utilizing Title I funding are given a great deal of flexibility in developing programs and initiatives that meet the needs of their parents (Borman, Stringfield, and Slavin 2001).

During the 1990s a new wave of educational changes emerged in the nation. More specifically, on April 18, 1991, two years after a national summit was held with the nation's governors to discussion the status of the country's public educational system, President George H. W. Bush revealed his comprehensive educational plan for the creation of national goals and standards by 2000. Not unlike most modern American presidents, he sought to reform the educational system as part of his platform.

The plan was sponsored jointly by the National Center on Education and the Economy and the Learning Research and Development Center at the University of Pittsburgh, and, similar to Reagan administration policy, partly sought to design a system of national exams that would improve the abilities of U.S. companies to compete in the international marketplace and partly aimed to improve the nature of public educational facilities throughout the nation. Also important was that several government officials of the Bush administration anonymously admitted that this plan was created to counter any criticism of the President's domestic agenda during the 1992 presidential campaign from various segments of the general population.

There were four main features of President Bush's education plan: (1) the creation of "model schools," (2) the development of national standards, (3) the creation of voluntary national achievement tests, and (4) the use of incentives for the construction of various school choice programs. The model schools program began on July 8, 1990, with the establishment of a private, nonprofit corporation known as *New American Schools Development Corporation (NASDC)*, which was funded with thousands of dollars of private corporate funds.

NASDC was also aided by the federal government in numerous unspoken and publically unknown ways. In short, the ultimate goal of the Bush administration, led by the NASDC, would be to develop approximately five hundred model schools, with one or two in each congressional district.

Simultaneously, the Bush administration also began to develop voluntary "American Achievement Tests" for grades four, eight, and twelve. These tests covered "core" subjects and student achievement was measured according to the results from an international perspective. To accomplish this goal, the administration, in connection with Congress and the National Governors Association, created the National Council on Education Standards and Testing (NCEST).

Similar to other reform proposals, the movement to create national standards also was strongly influenced by the American business community. For instance, the co-chairman of NCEST proclaimed that the main reason for the creation of national standards was to help middle and high school students compete in the world economy. In response to the proposal, as well as the comments of the co-chairman of NCEST, at the 1991 National Education Association annual conference, the organization voted to oppose any federally mandated national tests based on the view that the government eventually would try to control the develop of curriculum.

In the area of school choice, although the Reagan administration wanted to give parents an opportunity to choose between public and private schools for their children, the Bush administration, at least initially, supported only choice between public schools. However, in the later years of his tenure in the Oval Office, President Bush expanded his perspective also to include private schools. School choice became a major component of President Bush's educational plan because it could be used as a model school construct and also bridge the gap between public and private schools.

Finally, during the Bush administration and most of the early 1990s, there was a growing sentiment to create various choice programs and national standards, and to adopt some type of national testing for core subjects. However, since the mid-1990s, the standards movement has been transferred and transformed from the White House to the State House.

Subsequently, the task of the development of national standards and tests has been left up to professional organizations and curriculum specialists as well as state and local governments. For African American parents and students alike, the movement toward standardization, via standards, tests, and curriculum, which began in earnest during the 1990s, has led to an uneven and sometimes destructive impact on the educational experience of most persons of color who reside in urban school districts.

In 2002, Congress updated the ESEA by enacting No Child Left Behind (NCLB), inspired by the George W. Bush administration's pledge to reform education to meet the needs of all school-aged children. The ultimate goal of NCLB was to close the academic achievement gap present among U.S. elementary and secondary public school students. The achievement gap is best illustrated by the overwhelmingly higher achievement of white students over African American students on standardized tests, many of whom came from economically disadvantaged home and school environments. NCLB held great promise for those interested in the higher academic achievement of inner-city children.

NCLB updates provisions of Title I. Henderson and Mapp (2001) outlined six requirements all schools receiving Title I must follow:

1. All schools must develop a parent involvement policy with parents and approved by parents. This policy must include how it will build the school's capacity to engage families, address barriers to their involvement, and coordinate parent involvement in other programs.
2. Schools must notify parents and the community about this policy "in an understandable and uniform format " (76).
3. Schools must use at least 1 percent of the school's Title I funds to develop a parent involvement program. This money can be used for a wide range of activities—to hire parent liaisons, hold workshops and meetings, provide transportation and childcare, and make home visits.
4. Schools must describe and explain the school's curriculum, standards, and assessments.
5. Schools must develop a parent–school compact, or agreement, about how families and the school will collaborate to ensure children's progress.
6. Schools must give parents detailed information on student progress at the school.

Many schools follow some of the rules. Few follow the requirements completely. Without a staff member dedicated to parent involvement or a core of actively engaged parents, most of the required activities could easily be overlooked or given less priority over more immediate pressing issues.

NCLB has often been criticized as an "unfunded mandate." Effective parent involvement requires commitment of human and financial resources. Most public school systems are constantly being challenged with providing a greater level of service with less funding. More often than not, funding for any perceived outreach activities will get eliminated to make more resources for academic expenditures.

For example, at a large Midwestern inner-city school where the school only had enough money to hire either a guidance counselor or a librarian, the site council choose the librarian. Their rationale was that one librarian could service all two thousand students, but one counselor could impact only a fraction of them.

Most large urban school systems would need a dedicated parent involvement professional at the district level along with a specialist at the school level to enforce and oversee the Title I requirements. Somewhere in the system, perhaps as high as the federal government or perhaps through private financial support of public education, significant dollars must be allocated to support parent involvement at the professional level.

It is not enough to recruit and have strongly involved parents and expect to have continued parent involvement in the schools. Two specific examples come to mind. Roosevelt had an active parent named Kim (not her real name). She had two children in the school. Kim was always in the school, monitoring the halls, participating in school activities, or just hanging out in the parent center talking to teachers, staff, or other parents. She was also the PTO president.

Kim was impressive. She was a single parent, not working, totally dependent on public aid, and always casually dressed in jeans and a t-shirt or sweater. She was not particularly well spoken and used a great deal of slang in her speech. But she had a fervor, an enthusiasm about the school and her role as a parent leader. It was obvious that she cared about the children, the school, and the community. One day she was working in the courtyard picking up trash after recess. "We gotta keep this place clean," she said. "Set the example for the kids."

Kim attended school board meetings. She was part of a group of school and community leaders advocating for more qualified teachers at Roosevelt.

After a year of participating in the school, Kim disappeared. She had finally found a job and moved her family to what she described as a "safer neighborhood." She transferred the children to a school in their new community. While the job and move undoubtedly provided great benefits to Kim and her family, her departure was a huge loss for the school. Just like that, an active, fully engaged, motivated, inspirational, influential parent was gone.

Another situation occurred at Jefferson School (not its real name) that had a proactive parent named Karen (not her real name). She had a daughter in the third grade. Karen was a single parent working part-time. She always seemed to make time to participate in advocacy efforts on behalf of the school, regardless of her work schedule.

Karen was president of the PTA and participated with community organizers to oppose developers in the neighborhood surrounding the school. The school district had committed to building a new Jefferson School to replace the old dilapidated structure. Karen had worked tirelessly for months with other parents and school leaders on plans for the new school, including a new location that they felt would be safer for their children with respect to crime and traffic.

As Karen would later describe, those developers came in, and in one fell swoop, influenced the district to move the new school to a different location in the neighborhood. Karen joined community leaders in opposition to the school board and the developers, who she described as "being in bed together." A "highly charged" meeting took place at the school where developers and school board and administrators defended their actions to Karen and other parents and community members.

Karen spoke eloquently about the eight months of painstaking work she and others had participated in in the process of looking for a suitable location for the new school building. She talked about how the parents and school staff had become unified in their efforts to find the best location for the school in their poor neighborhood, and how she finally had hope for the future for the school and for her child. She said she hoped the school board would stand firm against "the mighty dollar." She and others believed the developers were promoting this move for some undisclosed financial gain to themselves.

Karen and the others had presented their position so well and the school board members appeared impressed. However, a few weeks later the school board decided in favor of the developers. Karen, heartbroken and disillusioned by the experience, responded by resigning her position as PTA president and withdrawing her daughter from Jefferson and enrolling her in a newly organized neighborhood charter school.

The point is, for a myriad of reasons, parents leave schools and take their children with them. They may have a change in life circumstances or become disgruntled or disillusioned in the school or the school system, or as ultimately happens in every case, their children naturally progress through the school system and graduate on to other schools. Developing, implementing, and sustaining parent involvement in schools is a continuous process. The resources have to be available to build a strong foundation that perpetuates parent involvement, regardless of which parents are involved.

It would be interesting to find out how many schools have actually developed a parent involvement policy in collaboration with parents. It would also be interesting to find out how many schools ever utilize the policy once it is completed. One parent served on the governance committee at his son's inner-city school. This school did not have an active parent specialist—one of the kindergarten teachers was assigned to coordinate parent-involvement activities. The father said that for the three years he served on the committee, they put together a parent involvement policy in the spring that fulfilled what appeared to be a requirement of the district, and never revisited it again during the school year.

Parents of children have the right, under the NCLB Act, to take their children out of failing schools and enroll them in performing schools in their district. Rarely did the parents of one large Midwestern urban school district take their children out of a failing school. That district has large numbers of supplementary educational service providers that give free tutoring to children from schools that are considered failing schools under NCLB. Parents of children in failing schools often would rather get the tutoring for their children than send them across town to another school in an unfamiliar neighborhood. And although it isn't discussed, often performing schools are not prepared to take transfer students because of capacity issues.

With the United States considered the greatest nation in the world, the expectation is that the American public education should be among the best in the world. Yet school-aged children in the United States consistently perform lower than their counterparts across the globe. With education being compulsory through age sixteen and all children having free access to education, you would think that U.S. children would outrank children in other countries in academic aptitude. Unfortunately, that is not the case.

The Programme for International Student Assessment (PISA) is the result of a collaborative effort between sixty-five countries and educational systems through the Organization for Economic Cooperation and Development. PISA conducted an assessment of fifteen-year-olds among the sixty-five countries and educational systems in 2009 (similar assessments have been done every three years starting in 2000; 2012 results were released in December 2013). The children were tested in three areas: math, reading, and science literacy. The United States had 5,233 participants. They ranked as follows: twenty-fifth in math, fifteenth in reading, and seventeenth in science. Considering that the United States is the most powerful nation in the world, the results are disturbing, and it is no wonder President Barack Obama has a different vision for the public education of children in America.

President Obama is one in a long line of presidents who pledged to improve the public education system and ensure that all children receive a quality education. His intentions appear well-meaning, but actual results remain to be seen. However, unlike his predecessor, President Obama has pledged substantial funding to support education. The new administration has established "Race to the Top," an initiative providing $4.35 million in competitive grants. States that develop initiatives around the following are considered for funding:

- Adopting standards and assessment that prepare students to succeed in college and the workplace and to compete in the global economy
- Building data systems that measure student growth and success, and inform teachers and principals about how they can improve instruction
- Recruiting, developing, rewarding, and retaining effective teachers and principals, especially where they are needed most
- Turning around our lowest achieving schools

President Obama has voiced strong support for charter schools, specifically those publicly funded institutions developed by a sponsor that are not subject to oversight by a school district but rather by a board of directors. This stance has been met with some criticism from traditional public school advocates, who see charter schools as a threat to public education by taking funding that could conceivably be used for traditional schools. More specifically, President Obama has been widely quoted regarding his position on parent involvement:

> There is no program or policy that can substitute for a mother or father who will attend those parent–teacher conferences or help with the homework or turn off the TV, put away the video games, read to their child. Responsibility for our children's education must begin at home. (State of the Union Address, February 24, 2009)

While President Obama's statement is correct, it appears to take some emphasis away from the responsibilities of schools to develop and implement parent involvement initiatives. One would argue that parent involvement is implied in the four areas specified in Race to the Top. The problem is that significant parent involvement often does not happen in schools without some urging by outside sources. The Race to the Top should have included a fifth area around parent involvement. That way we could be assured of the existence of fully developed initiatives focused on engaging parents in the educational process.

In all, the new administration has committed over $1 billion to support public education reforms. The president's aggressive push to improve education is very hopeful. Not in many years has a president really seemed to understand the core issues around the failure of public education to educate all children and actively taken on the task of turning around poor-performing schools. The discussion around creating national standards has not been given this much attention in years. It makes sense that in this global environment where we expect our children to ultimately thrive, we must ensure that they know where they stand with their peers.

HOW PRINCIPALS FEEL ABOUT PARENT INVOLVEMENT

Howard Kirschenbaum (2000) discussed his interviews with thirty-one school principals in Rochester, New York, City Schools regarding their feelings about parent involvement. His intent was to determine how school administrators feel about parent involvement, and if it is a priority for them. He said principals often described parents as "partners" and "allies" and virtually all the principals described parent involvement as "essential."

Kirschenbaum also talked about how important most of the principals felt a paid parent liaison in the school is to getting parents involved and how the district is moving toward having a full-time parent liaison in every Rochester public school. Placing the responsibility for parent engagement in the hands of a dedicated professional is an important first step.

Another reoccurring theme according to Kirschenbaum was the frustration of principals regarding poor parent attendance at school events. Principals also complained of the small number of rude, insulting, and sometimes violent parents who discourage school staff from seeking greater parent involvement. However, principals believe "their periodic successes with family engagement, the appreciative parent, the well-attended event, the enthusiastic volunteer, the growing sense of a school community, help remind them that the effort is worth it" (Kirschenbaum 2000, 29).

An education advocate conducted a survey in 2002 of thirty-seven elementary school principals in a large Midwestern city school district regarding parent involvement.[1] She was trying to gauge whether there was a correlation between academic achievement and the number of parents at a school who were involved as volunteers, in parent organizations, or on school governance councils.

The advocate (Parents for Public Schools) measured the academic achievement by the average number of students passing the state standardized test. The results supported the contention that parent involvement in the district resulted in increased student achievement. Of the top ten schools in performance on state tests, the average number of active PTO members was forty-two. Of the bottom ten schools, the average was nine. Of the top ten, the average number of parents serving on school governance councils was 5.5, compared with 1.9 for the lowest performing schools.

The advocate (Parents for Public Schools) discussed her survey results with the superintendent of schools. While the superintendent knew that parent involvement was a necessary and important component for schools, she seemed especially moved by the somewhat unscientific survey results. The district began to place more emphasis on outreach activities, hosting forums between parents and the superintendent, and placing more focus on parental concerns on school principals.

Eight of the ten bottom schools were inner-city schools. The other two schools, though located in middle class, residential neighborhoods, had large numbers of students from nearby low-income housing projects.

It is interesting to apply some statistics of Roosevelt School, discussed in chapter 1 and earlier in this chapter, to the results of this survey (Roosevelt was not part of the survey). Roosevelt had seven or eight consistently active PTO members, well below the forty-two in the top ten schools in the survey. Roosevelt had two parents on the school governance council, well below the 5.5 in the top ten schools. Roosevelt was an academically low performing school. Roosevelt's principal recognized that for Roosevelt to raise its academic level and have more high-performing students, he was going to have to find ways to make parents feel more welcome in the school, and he would have to help develop more effective communications and outreach between the school and parents.

DEFINITIONS AND DESCRIPTIONS OF PARENT INVOLVEMENT

To determine what parent involvement is requires an understanding of what constitutes a parent. Claire Smrekar and Lora Cohen-Vogel (2001) defined *parent* broadly to include the adult with responsibility for the financial and emotional care and support of the school-age child. That includes biological and adoptive parents and other designated family members such as grandparents, siblings, aunts, uncles, cousins, and foster parents.

The National Parent–Teacher Association (2000) referred to *parents* as any adults who play an important role in a child's upbringing and well-being. Peressini (1998) referred to *parenting* as the support that families provide for their children, ensuring their children's health and safety, developing parenting skills, creating child-rearing approaches that prepare children for school, maintaining healthy child development across grades, and building positive home conditions that support learning and behavior throughout the school years.

In comparison, scholar Dory Lightfoot (2004) views the term *parental involvement* as a "loaded," multifaceted, power-laden, and sometimes indefinable term.

Nevertheless, many seemingly equally important descriptions of parent involvement exist. Some see parent involvement occurring mainly at the school. Parent involvement has traditionally been defined as direct contact between school staff and parents, most frequently at school events, workshops, PTA meetings, and academic conferences (McKay, Atkins, Hawkins, Brown, and Lynn 2003). Kirschenbaum (2000) illustrates principals' perceptions of parent involvement by describing how they try to get more parents to join the PTA or PTO, recruit parents as volunteers, and maintain a full cadre of parents on the shared decision-making team.

While it is likely that most parents will have some reason to go to their child's school, whether it is for a school-sponsored event, a problem with the student, or as a volunteer, parent involvement is often considered an event that primarily occurs at home. Beaulieu and Granzin (1999) argue:

> Parent involvement means ensuring your child understands the value of education and the positive impact it will have in his or her life. Parent involvement also involves teaching your child to manage time effectively to include study time and to expect and work through difficult or seemingly impossible coursework. Parents should demonstrate genuine interest in their child's assignments and progress, develop good relationships with the child's teacher, structure a home life that is both educationally stimulating and supportive of the child's schoolwork, and demonstrate how important education is to the parent.

The involvement of parents in their children's education ideally should begin with preparing them for initial entry into school, and as children get older, parents should explain to them that it is important to go to school, let them know of the parents' expectations, check on their children's schoolwork and homework, and, if they can, assist with homework (Ogbu 2003).

Even the federal government has adopted an official definition of parent involvement:

> The statute defines parental involvement as the participation of parents in regular, two-way, and meaningful communication involving student academic learning and other school activities, including ensuring—
>
> - that parents play an integral role in assisting their child's learning;
> - that parents are encouraged to be actively involved in their child's education at school;
> - that parents are full partners in their child's education and are included, as appropriate, in decision-making and on advisory committees to assist in the education of their child; and
> - that other activities are carried out, such as those described in section 1118 of the ESEA (Parental Involvement). (ESEA, Section 9101[32])

Other activities as referred to in the statute involve the development and implementation of a written parent involvement policy in every school and in every school district. It appears that the definition of *parent involvement* is somewhat complex and multifaceted, and applies to individuals who are charged with the care and upbringing of children who are often not the birth parents. Parent involvement occurs at the school, at school-sponsored activities, as volunteers in the building, or on school governance councils and parent organizations. Parent involvement also occurs at different levels in the home, whether it is ensuring that children are properly reared so that they arrive at school ready to learn or whether they receive direct academic assistance from an adult in the home.

REFLECTIONS

Although much research exists to support the benefits of having parents involved in schools, it is a generally accepted principle that parents need to be involved in their children's education and in the schools. Many people can tell personal stories about the impact their parents have had on their education. Parents who are active in schools as volunteers also have positive influences on education.

Parent involvement is good for students and good for schools. The challenge is to create and sustain meaningful parent involvement in inner-city schools. That involves understanding how inner-city school environments differ from other school settings, and how to work through those differences to create positive results.

Obviously, there are compelling reasons to engage parents in the educational process. Unsatisfactory academic achievement is a prevailing issue in many inner-city schools. Pursuing active, consistent, and sustained parent involvement in education appears to provide benefits to schools and children. Schools with large numbers of academically struggling children especially need to place significant focus on developing strategies to get parents into the school buildings and to get them to focus on education while children are at home. Parents should also focus on making sure that children get enough food and rest, and are mentally prepared to give their best efforts while in school.

NOTE

1. This information used for this claim was obtained and synthesized but never published by a local parent advocacy group known as "Parents for Public Schools" that operated during the early 2000s. The primary purpose of the organization was to pressure the local school district to improve the test scores of its students as well as increase the avenues for parental involvement.

THREE

Types of Parents

The "traditional" family usually has a mother and father who are married and living together in the same home with their children. Many of these traditional families have a mother who does not work outside the home. Others have two working parents. Fifty years ago, such a family would be classified as the norm. Today there are many variations on the parent and family theme. This chapter highlights several types of "parents" prevalent in inner-city schools.

SINGLE PARENTS

Single parenthood dominates the family situation in urban school settings. In 2007, an estimated 13.7 million single parents had custody of 21.8 million children under twenty-one years of age while the other parent lived somewhere else. Mothers accounted for 82.6 percent of custodial parents and 17.4 percent were fathers

More recently, Don Eberly, founder and CEO of the National Fatherhood Initiative, calls fatherhood absence a national epidemic, indicating that nearly 40 percent of children in America (twenty-four million) go to bed in a home in which their natural father does not live. According to Mr. Eberly, children from father-absent homes are:

- Five times more likely to live in poverty
- Three times more likely to fail in school
- Two to three times more likely to develop emotional or behavioral problems
- Three times more likely to commit suicide

Please rephrase this sentence to state "Inner city schools are full of children living in poverty. More importantly this same children are more likely to attended substandard public schools, compared to their suburb counterparts." With children in these situations more likely to fail in school, educators in inner-city schools must understand the additional challenges of having large numbers of children from single-parent households.

There is a mounting concern about the number of households without fathers. In June of 2001, President George W. Bush, speaking at the National Fatherhood Initiative's Fourth Annual National Summit on Fatherhood in Washington, D.C., said the following:

> Over the past four decades, fatherlessness has emerged as one of our greatest social problems. We know that children who grow up with absent fathers can suffer lasting damage. They are more likely to end up in poverty or drop out of school, have a child out of wedlock, or end up in prison. Fatherlessness is not the only cause of these things, but our nation must recognize it is an important factor.

Single-parent households are probably the majority family structure in many inner-city school environments. Some households are headed by working parents with a single full- or part-time income. Others may be receiving some kind of government aid. Single parents raising school-aged children often do not have the built-in support systems of a two-parent family. They may not have another adult that can cover childcare, transportation, supervision, or a second income for expenses. Many single parents work very hard, sometimes to their own detriment in terms of leisure time, health issues, finances, and personal and professional goals to ensure the success of their children in school.

Macy has two children, one in the third grade and one in eleventh grade. She is a single mother working full-time as a city bus driver. Her children's fathers do not live in the home, and have limited to no contact with her and the children.

Being a single parent was a struggle from the beginning. Macy had to remove her youngest child from one school because bus service from her home was canceled due to budget cuts. She enrolled her in a school that was in the inner-city neighborhood where they lived, and where she did not need bus service. Macy has received a lot of help from friends and church members because her daughters are involved in afterschool activities.

Macy regrets she has little time to spend on parent involvement at her children's schools. Her work schedule allows her little time to visit the school or attend PTO meetings. Recently, she took a second job part-time in the evenings to bring in more money to sustain their modest household. Her seventeen-year-old recently took a job working in a restaurant ten hours per week during the school year, which enables her to have her own spending money, to Macy's delight.

Artie is a single father with two girls in elementary school. He works a first-shift job at a plant, but gets up early each morning to get his girls fed and ready for school. He takes them to school at 7:15 a.m. and then goes straight to work. The girls stay at school for an afterschool program and Artie picks them up every day around 4:30 p.m.

Artie's ex-girlfriend, the girls' mother, is on crack and is not actively part of their lives, seeing the girls occasionally on holidays. He often expresses concern about being able to successfully raise his girls to be strong, educated young women. Artie is a high school graduate, but never pursued college, and was never a strong student.

Ken was never married to his daughter Kendra's mother. Kendra's mother had other children with other fathers. When Kendra was about ten, she went to live with Ken across town. Ken was all for being a full-time dad, but had to get accustomed to the changes in his routine.

Ken was accustomed to waking up for work at 7:30 a.m. and grabbing a donut on the way so that he could get there by 8:30 a.m. With Kendra in the house, he now had to wake up at 6:15 a.m., make sure she was awake and getting ready as they had to share one bathroom, make breakfast, pack a lunch for her, and make sure she got to school on time at 8 a.m., while getting to work on time himself.

Since Kendra's school was located just outside the one-mile radius to qualify for bus service, Ken took her to school, which was in the opposite direction of his job. He had to make arrangements for her to attend an after-school program until he could pick her up after work and make sure he had dinner for her, and he had an alternate plan if school was not in session. This was quite a transition for a busy single man living alone.

Single parents span all ages. One local elementary principal talked about how she was starting to see the children of students she remembered getting pregnant as twelve- and thirteen-year-olds. Two girls in particular, who were promising teens, got pregnant around the same time and had children in the pre-K class. One of the girls dropped out of high school and was living with her mother and working a part-time job to help make ends meet. The other girl stayed in school, and though she was slightly behind the rest of her graduating class, she estimated that it would not be long before she graduated and enrolled in community college.

GRANDPARENTS

With single-parent families being so prevalent in inner-city schools, there is crossover with other family situations. A prime example is the number of single grandparents raising grandchildren. While there are grandparents in their late twenties and thirties, many retirement-age grandparents are raising small children.

According to the 2000 U.S. Census, 2.4 million grandparents were raising grandchildren. Newly released data from the 2010 census indicates 4.9 million children under eighteen live in grandparent-headed households. Approximately 20 percent of these grandparents are raising their grandchildren without the help or presence of the parents. Many of these children are attending inner-city schools.

According to a 2011 report completed by the American Academy of Child and Adolescent Psychiatry, most grandchildren move in with grandparents for one of the following reasons:

- Increasing numbers of single-parent families
- The high rate of divorce
- Incarcerations of parents
- Substance abuse by parents
- Illness, disability, or death of parents
- Parental abuse or neglect

One grandparent indicated that her child was too irresponsible, dropping her grandchild off with her and disappearing for a few days (Gladstone and Brown 2002). The daughter's irresponsibility led to the grandmother ultimately legally seeking and receiving full custody of her grandchild.

Ms. Edwards is raising two grandchildren. She says her daughter is currently not responsible and she was worried about the children's welfare so she took them into her home permanently. One child is seven years old and is mental retarded and developmentally disabled. The other is in seventh grade in a charter school.

Ms. Edwards and her husband are young grandparents in their late forties, working blue collar jobs and making decent salaries. At this point, they are not receiving money to support their grandchildren. "Our daughter is out in the streets right now," she regretted. "We're comfortable (financially) but we had plans to retire early so we may put that off for awhile."

Unlike Ms. Edwards, who is a relatively young grandparent who works and earns a respectable living, many grandparents may not have the income they had as working adults, which may place a strain on their family as they attempt to raise their grandchildren. One grandmother talked about how the money she had saved for retirement was now helping to pay for the four grandchildren she was raising (Lawrence-Webb, Okundaye, and Hafner 2003). Most grandparents plan to spend some money buying gifts or other items for their grandchildren, but likely few to none plan their finances or retirement so that they can afford to raise their grandchildren.

With aging comes health and healthcare issues. Grandparents raising children often have to deal with their own challenges as well. Smrekar and Cohen-Vogel (2001) conducted a study of family involvement in a Northern California public elementary school in a low-income community. Among the "parents" studied were two grandmothers raising grandchildren. Both referred to health problems, such as back trouble and arthritis, that limited their mobility and hindered their ability to leave their home occasionally. If they could not leave their homes, they could not participate in parent teacher conferences, Parent–Teacher Association (PTA) or Organization (PTO) meetings, or other meetings or activities in their grandchildren's schools, although they could possibly provide support from home.

Ms. Gibson has a son in the sixth grade and a granddaughter in the first grade. Her situation is interesting. She has two young children to care for, one being a child that she had at a later age (mid-forties), along with her granddaughter. And Ms. Gibson is single. Her daughter is not present in their household and is not contributing financially or emotionally to the living situation.

One grandmother who lives in the local inner city is in a wheelchair, yet she raises her teenaged granddaughter who is in high school and who has a small child herself. The student's mother is not actively or consistently involved in her daughter's life.

Some grandparents are very young, and aren't necessarily ready to be grandparents. An example is the grandmother who is thirty-four years old with a fifteen-year-old son who has a toddler himself. The grandmother is divorced and has a very active social life, so the fifteen-year-old, his girlfriend (the toddler's mother), and the toddler spend the majority of their time with the grandmother's mother, great-grandmother to the toddler.

Some community organizations offer support, or at least an opportunity for grandparents to unwind and to vent. A local educator also works in the evenings facilitating a grandparent support group. She reports that school-related issues of custodial grandchildren often dominate group discussions. They talk about issues such as having to attend school meetings regarding disciplinary actions; needing extra money for clothes, food, and supplies; and the frustrations of trying to help children with schoolwork.

The grandparents share their experiences, triumphs, and frustrations; provide advice to one another; and help each other research solutions to some of their issues and concerns. The facilitator often invites guest speakers, such as attorneys, social workers, psychologists, and other specialists that answer questions and give guidance to the grandparents.

One of the greatest challenges of raising children in low-income communities is having the money to meet their basic needs and still have money to maintain the household. As opposed to foster parents, grandparents do have the advantage that they often already have the love relationship that comes from kinship. However, public assistance across the country does not have a consistent approach to allotting money for custodians of children. Often foster care providers are eligible for more money and benefits than grandparents. One grandmother indicated that her cash assistance award for being a grandmother custodian was about $250 per month, while foster care parents get $700 to $800 per month (Huplip and Patrick 2006).

The manner in which cash assistance is granted to foster parents versus grandparents or others with a kinship to the child varies from state to state. The funding funnels through the federal government to state agencies, who use different levels of discretion in allotting money to custodians. In some cases the custodial care of children by grandparents and other blood relatives may be considered part of the family's responsibility, and thus should not be compensated, or at least not as generously as the care of a nonrelated guardian. Other states may treat a custodial situation with more equity.

In the inner-city environment, where there are situations of limited family income, the issue of cash assistance for raising a grandchild can have a significant effect on the level of involvement a grandparent can have in the child's school. In the case of a grandparent who is receiving a small cash award for raising a grandchild, it may be necessary for that grandparent to hold part-time or full-time employment, or take an extra job if he or she is already working. That could take time away from otherwise available time for parent involvement.

Many grandparents do become active in the schools. An active grandmother once mentioned that being retired, she had more time to spend volunteering at the school and attending school activities than she did when she was working, and wanted to do a better job at school involvement for her grandchildren than she had done for her children.

The fact is, grandparents raising children is becoming more and more common in school environments, especially in the city. Some have legal custody of the children and others just take care of their grandchildren for significant periods of time. Educators are becoming more and more aware of the need to be able to effectively interact with grandparents to the benefit of students.

OTHERS RAISING CHILDREN

There are situations where people other than parents or grandparents have the responsibility for the care of children. These can be other family members, such as aunts, uncles, siblings, or cousins, or they could be foster or adoptive parents. They sometimes have formal or legal agreements, or they may just be raising the child or children while the parent is unavailable, incapable, or unwilling to raise them.

Ms. Jordan was raising a niece in the first grade. Her niece performed poorly in school and Ms. Jordan spent much time at the school meeting with the principal because of the child's disciplinary problems. She expressed the challenges of raising a niece with learning disabilities and a serious behavioral problem. She spent many hours at the school in consultation with teachers and staff, and they managed her niece's situation using an individualized educational plan.

One lady, a full-time college student, adopted her young nephews after they were left parentless. Both boys are in elementary school. She is also unmarried and single.

Another woman adopted two sisters from the same family. She is not related to the children, but is a close friend of the family. The young parents were not interested in raising the children at that time and the grandmother was ill and unable to care for them. The woman struggled with having enough money and received no support from the family, save a few dollars here and there from the grandmother. She also had failing health herself, but she managed to get both girls, teenagers at the time of adoption, through high school and into college.

Ms. Betty and Mr. Bill lived in the inner city of a large Midwestern city. They have raised many foster children in their home in addition to their own two children. They describe their situation with their family as "blessed," and want to give back by allowing less-fortunate children to have the same experiences they had.

A single mother of five took in her brother's four children. He was working out of town and could not keep them. All the children were school aged except for one who was in her first year of college.

Sometimes a parental situation involves a noncustodial parent. An inner-city school hosted a "Donuts for Dads" activity. About twenty fathers showed up at the event, which many of the teachers reportedly assumed would be unsuccessful. The parent coordinator gave flyers to teachers to distribute to the students, who were to deliver them to their fathers. According to the parent coordinator, some teachers were so cynical about the fathers' interest in their children that they did not give the flyers to the students. Many were pleased at the turnout. Most of the fathers present did not live with their children, but were eager to be involved in the educational process. One father expressed a concern that he was not always informed about his school affairs because all the information went to his child's mother.

PARENTS WITH DISABILITIES AND OTHER PHYSICAL CONDITIONS

Some parents have disabilities that hinder their ability to get around. Others have health conditions, such as mental health or substance abuse issues that limit their ability to be as active in school as they would like.

A principal once wondered why the mother of one of his most behaviorally challenged students never came to the school. He later found out that she was a single parent confined to a wheelchair, which limited her mobility. He was able to set up regular phone meetings with the mother to discuss her son.

Ms. Ronan, a school nurse, had worked in inner-city schools for nearly twenty years. She talked with parents who admitted to her that they had mental illness problems. In many cases, a parent would be genuinely concerned about how his or her condition affected the child in school.

Martha was the mother of a third grade son with behavioral challenges. She had always had emotional problems, being prone to sudden outbursts and panic attacks that she controlled with medication. She was always concerned that her outbursts were the cause for her son's behavior, and while the possibility existed that her condition was a contributing factor, there were other issues present. They were in and out of homeless shelters and temporary housing. Martha did not graduate from high school and did not have a GED, so she had challenges finding consistent and meaningful work. The boy had asthma and was not always well.

Ms. Moore, a school social worker, interacted with parents distressed about their circumstances. In over five hundred home visits per year, she encountered many parents suffering from depression. "Many can't see a better day; not enough food, horrible surroundings," she said. "Some parents are so depressed they could not get out of bed."

Ms. Moore saw many instances of substance abusing parents of children in inner-city schools. One mother who was a drug addict had a very promising son who always performed well academically. Ms. Moore bought the boy a new outfit from her own pocket to wear to his eighth grade graduation. She lamented that she made the mistake of leaving the tags on the clothes. The boy did not attend graduation and later admitted that his mother returned the items to the store and used the money to buy drugs.

A principal of an inner-city school enforced a dress code in her school—no shorts until May. She contended that once the weather got warm and children started wearing less formal attire to school, they were less serious about their studies and their behavior.

One day she noticed that for the third day straight, a third grade boy wore the same pair of shorts. She decided to walk the boy home after school and talk to his mother about his attire, since he lived across the street from the school. When they got to his home, they found his mother, who appeared to be under the influence of some controlled substance, sitting on the couch incoherent and unresponsive. The principal went into Jimmy's bedroom to help him find some pants to wear, and what she saw was a stack of dirty clothes that were piled up to the ceiling. Feeling sorry for the boy, she decided to give him some outfits from the extra clothes they kept at the school. She worried about that boy, knowing that he was probably left most days to care for himself.

BLENDED FAMILIES

Some children are living in some very complicated blended-family circumstances. Blended families ultimately form after one or both sides have experienced some sort of separation or loss. Parents have experienced divorce, breakup, or death. The parents and the children are dealing with changes and perhaps unresolved emotions. While some blended situations may be positive, others family situations may be more difficult for children to function within on both a short-term and long-term basis.

Jane lives in a small house in the inner city of a large Midwestern city with her father, his girlfriend, and her grandparents, along with children of her father and girlfriend. Her mother lives across town with her husband and their children.

Another child lives with her mother and her mother's boyfriend. Her father is deceased. She has three siblings, and the boyfriend has children of his own that often visit the household.

There are some complex parental situations in inner-city schools in close-knit neighborhoods. One local school has a number of sets of children who are siblings with one common parent. For example, three children close in age may have the same mother, but different fathers or the same father but different mothers. It is understandable how that can be confusing in the school setting to all involved. One local school administrator explained that in her school they have several situations where the dad is father to four or five children with different mothers, some of whom do not want their children in the same classroom or do not want the dad to have access to the child, making complex issues for the school regarding access.

PARENTS AND EMPLOYMENT

Nonworking parents of students are ever-present in inner-city schools. One parent said that while she agreed that her children's school needed more active parent support, she wasn't interested in volunteering at the school because she had to find a job to feed her three children. A father was concerned about supporting his family because both he and his wife were on disability from their respective jobs, therefore receiving limited monthly incomes. Another single mother with two small children was worried because she'd just been laid off from her factory job at a company a couple of blocks from the school.

Underemployment is also an issue with families in the inner city. Many single mothers are working at minimum wage jobs raising multiple children. One mother said that with no education, all she could find was a part-time job working in a daycare center while her three children were in school.

Many inner-city parents see opportunities to earn higher wages by finding employment located long distances from their homes. Ms. Moore, the school social worker, said that many working parents in the inner city who do not own cars catch buses to get better paying jobs in the suburbs, which makes for "long days if they have to work outside the city—ten- to twelve-hour days because they don't have cars. You wouldn't believe some of the situations some of these mothers go through to get to work. Some don't get home until three o'clock in the morning." Many of them catch two or more buses to get to work. In some situations, parents without a car ride the bus with their small children to drop them off with family members, then catch another bus and sometimes two to get to work. After work, those same parents ride the bus back to the family member's house, pick up their children, and ride the bus home.

Ms. Moore also talked about parents who obtained decent paying full-time jobs working second and third shift, but slept most of the day and didn't have time to come to the school. Often, she said, their children were late to school or even absent because their parents were asleep and could not wake them in time. Ms. Moore noted the number of late children everyday, and knowing their situations, gave out alarm clocks to fifty students to assist them in getting up in the morning and getting to school on time. She noted that most of the children started getting to school on time as a result of getting the alarm clocks.

Some parents worked early morning shifts and had to leave the house for work before their children woke up or left for school. One Roosevelt parent expressed her concerns about her nine-year-old daughter having to wake herself up, bathe and feed herself, and walk several blocks past the drug dealers and across a main thoroughfare to get to school every day. But she had no choice—she had to make a living to pay the rent and buy food.

Ms. Moore recalled seeing many more parents in the school buildings when public aid was more readily available. "When AFDC [Aid to Families with Dependent Children] was available, more parents were home during the day and could come to the school. Now, many are scratching a living," she said. AFDC, which was formerly called "welfare," consisted of monthly cash payments to low-income families. AFDC was replaced in the late 1990s by Temporary Assistance for Needy Families (TANF). TANF provides temporary financial assistance to low-income families for a specified period. Adults receiving TANF assistance are expected to pursue job opportunities or go to school to train for jobs to continue to receive the assistance. As a result of TANF, millions of parents nationwide who were formerly unemployed and receiving monthly welfare payments are now working, but again, if the jobs are low paying, part-time, or seasonal, parents struggle to make ends meet.

Ms. Thompson, a parent involvement coordinator, felt a responsibility to help parents get jobs if possible, or at least alert them to possible job opportunities. She received several complaints from parents about the lack of crossing guards on some of the streets surrounding the school. She did some investigation and found that the city hires and pays crossing guards. She also found out that in the immediate vicinity of the school, the city indicated they were three crossing guards short. So she requested the job posting from the city and posted it in the parent center. Several parents applied for the positions and at least one was hired.

PARENTS IN SCHOOL

Some parents are in school. This occurrence is even more common now with the ending of AFDC, or welfare. More mothers are pursuing academic or vocational training to prepare for careers. One parent who had a couple of children at Roosevelt who admitted she had behavioral problems lamented about the number of college classes she missed and ultimately had to drop because of meetings she had to attend at school because of her children's issues. She was concerned that she might never finish school. Her dream was to finish nursing school so that she could get a better paying job to support her family.

Community colleges and career academies have large numbers of parents of school-aged children in school themselves. Many parents are laid off and in retraining for some new career. Many who were formerly solely dependent on public assistance are in school to pursue careers in fields such as nursing, early childhood education, massage therapy, and other health- and business-related programs.

Parents who are in school are looking for other options. Several are attracted to the online learning environment. But without the ability to obtain computers, the challenge becomes where to get homework done. Public libraries have a limited number of computers with limits on how long an individual can use one before it's someone else's turn. Colleges are providing more computer labs and various studies show that adult learners are doing much of their online coursework at computers on campus. However, many parents still do not have time to go on the campuses, or even to the library. Some mothers who are fortunate enough to have jobs where they use a computer may have an opportunity to do some homework at lunchtime, but that is usually not enough time to finish schoolwork.

REFLECTIONS

This is a sampling of some of the types of family arrangements found in inner-city schools. The most important point to take from this chapter is that there is no one typical family in an inner-city school. When planning outreach and activities involving parents, their individual circumstances need to be taken into account to ensure maximum success.

FOUR

Barriers to Effective Parent Involvement

Everyone talks about how important parent involvement is to the success of elementary and secondary schools. Researchers have shown through numerous studies the positive effects that active and sustained parent engagement have on the education of children. However, effective parent involvement is difficult to achieve. In the chapter, we seek to explore this dilemma.

UNFRIENDLY SCHOOLS

According to many studies and some anecdotal claims, the most prevalent reason why thousands of parents are not involved in their children's education endeavors is because they see the schools as unfriendly. For example, Bowles and Gintis (Bowles and Gintis 1976) claimed in one of the earliest studies on this topic that parental involvement differs based on the social class in which they serve. As a result, the involvement of parents in a particular school will be different based if it is located in a working-class or middle-class neighborhood. Many school systems strive for parent-friendly schools that are welcoming to families and the communities of which they are a part. An analysis of unfriendly schools falls best under three categories: physical appearance of school buildings, personal contact with parents, and telephone communications. Each of these descriptions represent an initial point of contact, which, if unpleasant, is often enough to turn away a frustrated parent. These points are discussed first.

PHYSICAL APPEARANCE OF SCHOOL BUILDINGS

For parents concerned about their children's educational experiences, there is nothing more unappealing than some of the school buildings that are out there today, particularly in the inner city. While the characteristics of an unwelcome school vary from schoolhouse to schoolhouse, there are some distinct characteristics of unfriendly schools. Many buildings are decades-old institutions. Indeed, many of these older buildings that were constructed in the early 1900s and older look like factories, cold and scary, with large heavy doors.

Even some school buildings constructed in the 1950s through the 1970s look like businesses or institutions rather than schoolhouses. Many are in need of repairs or renovations, having not been constructed for long-term usage or energy efficiency. One school district in a large Midwestern city is in the process of rebuilding or renovating nearly all of the school buildings, and most of the newer buildings built in the 1950s, 1960s, and 1970s have been demolished and rebuilt.

Many schools are unkempt. Litter and broken glass clutter the grounds. Some school buildings have more blue replacement windows than the clear glass windows, making them unsightly. Many have maintenance problems inside and out. Some buildings have buckets situated in classrooms or in the hall, catching dripping water when it rains. Others have bathrooms with nonworking commodes or faucets. One local school had one working girls bathroom, with one of the three toilets working in a school populated by six hundred students from pre-K through eighth grade. The water in the faucet was cold. There was no hot water in the building for children to wash their hands, and the soap dispenser was broken.

Several factors within the school, actually in the office, can influence someone's assessment of whether or not the school is friendly. For example, in *Engaging All Families* (2003), Dr. Steven Constantino described his first experience in the office on his first day as the new principal at Stonewall Jackson High School in Manassas, Virginia. He noticed the worn carpet, mismatched plastic chairs lined up against the wall, the clocks that didn't tell the correct time, the years of neglect, the mismatched filing cabinets, the old wood student desks used to prop up typewriters and the counter. He experienced the kinds of things prevalent in many inner-city schools.

He described a fifteen-foot long counter, over which he could see the tops of the heads of two office staff persons (Constantino 2003, 16). After what seemed like a few minutes of waiting and clearing his throat to get someone's attention, he finally said, "Good morning," to which one of the ladies replied, "Yes?" He replied, "I am the new principal." She replied," Oh, your office is over there," pointing to a vacant office. She immediately went back to whatever she was doing.

Dr. Constantino recalled wondering how everyone who came to the office was treated. He recalled thinking that what the school was really saying was, "Welcome to our broken-down school where we hope we will make you feel as if you are imposing on us. Please take a seat in the mismatched uncomfortable plastic chairs while we decide if we are going to help you or not" (Constantino 2003, 17).

Dr. Constantino acknowledged that ultimately the school replaced the carpet and furniture. But most importantly, to his delight, they removed the counter, which he signified as the greatest physical barrier to visitors. In that school culture, the counter was the symbol of unfriendliness. A good way to start the process toward a more friendly school is to identify the symbolic barrier or barriers to parent involvement, and remove them. Other examples of such symbolic barriers could be uncomfortable seating, including child-size chairs for adults and an unfriendly receptionist.

Sometimes finding the entrance to the building is a challenge. Many schools have multiple doors. A parent can go to what he or she thinks is the right door, and find it locked. The actual entrance is on the other side of the building. School buildings should have clear signage that directs visitors to the entrance if it is not clearly visible. In some older buildings, the name of the school is carved in stone or in some way built into the structure, but doesn't necessarily delineate the school entrance. In those cases, perhaps standing signs positioned in high-traffic areas would be more helpful to parents and other visitors.

Lack of welcoming signage is prevalent in many schools. Even once in the building, sometimes finding the office or any other room in the building can be confusing, even intimidating to a parent. Parents have wandered around school buildings desperately looking for the office or the library or lunchroom or some other room, with no clue as to where to go, and no signage that gives any indication of where their destination is. Trying to figure out where to go in the building can be frustrating for a parent who may have limited time to visit a school, or even someone who is just anxious to get to where he or she is going. An experience like that could make a parent never want to come back to the school.

PERSONAL CONTACT

It is frustrating for parents to go into a school building and be ignored, or not be asked if they could be helped or directed. In some schools parents must walk past adults working in the building who ignore them, don't notice them, or just don't want to speak to them, or so it seems. Even if the intent is not to be rude and unfriendly, allowing someone to wander around the building without acknowledging them or helping them is definitely not inviting to a visitor.

One of the most aggravating experiences in unfriendly schools is going into the office and getting poor service from receptionists and other staff. A superintendent in the large urban Midwestern school district told the story of how he, as the new superintendent, went into a school office and waited at least five minutes while the office staff ignored him and continued a conversation they were having. Of course the two ladies were embarrassed and apologetic when they finally discovered they had ignored the new superintendent, but the damage was already done. And there is no telling how many frustrated parents had been ignored prior to the superintendent.

An unfriendly and unwelcoming atmosphere may be the most significant barrier to parents, particularly those who had unpleasant or unsuccessful educational experiences as children. Quite frankly, no parent, regardless of status, appreciates being treated poorly at their child's school. There is no greater frustration for a parent than to go to the school office and be ignored and treated as though he or she is intruding on the receptionist's time.

TELEPHONE COMMUNICATIONS

Obviously initial contact between parents and schools is a strong indicator of a school's welcoming nature. The manner in which the phone is answered in some schools is an immediate turnoff for parents. When parents called "Adams High School" to set up a meeting with the principal about an upcoming parent-outreach event the school was sponsoring, the receptionist answered the phone, "Adams"—not "Adams High School," or "Adams High School. How may I help you?" or anything even close. She just gave a very abrupt response of "Adams." Parents who have to speak with someone will grudgingly wait, while others would hang up in frustration.

Some parents call a school and get put on hold with no explanation. The phone call will go something like this: "Hello, this is Madison School, please hold," and with no chance to acknowledge, the parent is immediately put on hold. Some parents hang up right there.

Schools can get hectic, with situations like children needing assistance, parents and visitors coming into the building, and the normal passing of classes and lunch periods, to name a few examples. Parents can probably understand the chaos of a school office, but at least deserve the courtesy of having someone get back to them after a few minutes to make a polite gesture, such as "I'm sorry for your wait, and someone will be with you shortly!"

GENERAL COMMUNICATIONS

Communication between parents and schools is often an indicator of barriers to parent involvement. Many parents feel misinformed about situations involving their children. Parents complain they do not get any notification of academic or behavioral problems, or even absences of their children until they see their report card.

Ms. Jordan said that she sometimes heard about problems her niece had had in school two weeks after the situation happened. She found out her niece had skipped school after seeing the absences on her report card. Ms. Bothwell, another parent, complained that her child's school should do a better job publicizing the Parent–Teacher Organization (PTO) meetings and other school-sponsored events. "We usually don't get notification about PTO meetings until it is too late. If we could get the information a week before, I could make plans to go," she said. "But they usually send the information out a day or two ahead of time."

Usually that kind of information is sent by flyer home with the children. One teacher at an inner-city school said that she would often find flyers out on the playground after school or in the garbage cans. To ensure that parents of her students received information, she often sent flyers, report cards, and other messages via U.S. mail at her own expense.

Parents need time to prepare for when school will not be in session. The school should not always depend on parents to remember days that school is not in session. One parent complained that the school was closed for an in-service day, and she knew nothing about it until her child told her in the morning that she didn't have to go to school that day. The parent had no childcare plans for her young child, and was lucky to have an employer who allowed her to take a vacation day on short notice.

Not every parent has the option of having an understanding employer or a quick solution to a daycare dilemma. Several parents of middle school children in a large Midwestern city participated with a focus group sponsored by a nonprofit organization, and mothers lamented about the number of times they had to leave their children at home alone while they went to work because they did not receive adequate notice to make childcare arrangements. Others spoke of losing jobs or jeopardizing their employment for having to call off at the last moment to stay home with a child.

Some parents wish they could get good news about their children sometime, instead of bad news about academics or behavior. One father said, "I know my kids are doing something right. I wish I could hear something positive about my kids."

SCHEDULING

It is probably not possible to accommodate the schedule of every parent when planning school activities. Parents who work or are in school may have limited time to come to their children's schools. Parents who work during the day may only be available after 5 p.m. or 6 p.m. Some parents who work swing shifts like 11 a.m. through 8 p.m. or second-shift jobs cannot attend afternoon school events. Others may work night-shift jobs and sleep during the day.

Some administrators try to help parents overcome the time barrier. Take the case of Dr. Jones at Roosevelt School, who had so many mothers walking their children to school in the morning that he decided to schedule the PTO meeting at 8 a.m. He instructed the lunchroom staff to serve a full-course breakfast to attract the mothers to stay. They went from having three to five parents at a PTO meeting at 3 p.m. to having twenty to twenty-five parents in an 8 a.m. breakfast meeting.

Parent–teacher conferences are often not well attended in inner-city schools. Again, some parents complain that they get late notification about conferences, and that the times they are given to choose from do not fit their schedules. One principal tried to accommodate all schedules once by inviting parents to come to the school one day anytime between 8 a.m. and 8 p.m. to meet with teachers on an in-service day. It was a risk, partly because of concerns involving the teachers' union contract, which limits the time teachers can work each day.

The principal reported little resistance from teachers, who were anxious to talk to parents, and he agreed to give some flexible schedule times to teachers as compensation. The school did experience some improvement in conference attendance; about 50 percent of parents attended. In a school of about four hundred students, it was better than some conference days, where less than twenty parents total would show up for conferences.

UNFAVORABLE EDUCATIONAL EXPERIENCES OF PARENTS

Many parents associate coming into a school with their own adverse educational experiences. Parents who dropped out of school or were not the best students may not have a strong comfort level in dealing with teachers or other professionally trained school staff.

One parent acknowledged that she would only step foot in her son's school in case of emergency because she "hated" school as a child. Another parent of an elementary school student who was thirteen when she gave birth admitted that she found it difficult to go into her son's school because many of the teachers who were there when she got pregnant and quit school were still there.

Other parents said they just did not enjoy school because they did not have any friends or were teased for some reason or another. Some said they just did not feel comfortable around teachers and would not come into the school.

USE OF EDUCATIONAL JARGON

Parent discomfort in talking with teachers and school administrators is often compounded by the use of educational jargon that may not be understandable to parents. Kinnaman (2002) is one of many educator–authors who suggests that educators do not really seem to want parents involved. He refers to teachers who talk educational jargon that most parents don't understand. Examples like *project-centered, learner-centered, aligned with standards,* and the *scientific method* are terms that often confuse parents. While educators do not necessarily want to confuse parents, phrases that are common to educators and not to parents give an impression that they really do not care if the parents understand what they are talking about, or that they really do not want them to understand.

Educational jargon is especially difficult for parents who struggle with reading. Mr. Dunn, the father of three children at an inner-city elementary school, admitted to me that he had difficulty reading correspondence that came from the school, and usually let his wife handle those communications.

Educational jargon often gets used in individualized education plan (IEP) meetings. Often parents, particularly those without an advocate in the meeting, can feel very intimidated by the various discussions going on. Many parents skip the meetings all together.

UNSAFE NEIGHBORHOODS

Sometimes unsafe or crime-laden neighborhoods are a serious deterrent to active and sustained parent involvement. One mother lived right down the street from the inner-city school her daughters attended. She was saving money to move out of the neighborhood. She walked her two young children to and from school everyday past what she described as drug dealers, pimps, prostitutes, and criminals.

When the girls got home after school, they stayed in the house the rest of the evening. She regretted that her children could not go outside and play because of the sound of gunshots in the neighborhood nearly every evening. She told me she was not comfortable coming back to the school for evening events, and usually would not attend them.

It is truly a shame that so much crime and violence happens in the vicinity of schools. Parents send their children to schools with the hope and assurance that they are in safe environments. Many cities have shootings, rapes, and robberies within a one-block radius of some of schools. What a burden for parents!

A city councilman in a large urban Midwestern city had a private discussion with some parents who described the drug and prostitution activity immediately surrounding their children's school. The parents were grateful that he had taken the time to speak with them. The council-man thanked the parents for their time and seemed to care about their concerns. However, parents claim to have not seen any significant in-crease in a police presence in the vicinity of the school. Most of the par-ents had little faith in the system, assuming that their neighborhood would always be neglected regardless of the physical closeness of crime to the neighborhood school.

DON'T KNOW HOW TO GET INVOLVED

Sometimes parents want to be involved but they just do not know how to become an active parent in their child's educational experience. Ms. Cun-ningham, the mother of a seventh grader, fourth grader, and second grader, said she would like to see teachers do a better job of engaging parents. "Teachers should try to call parents to invite them to the school," she said. "They should send home better instructions on how parents can help their children."

Another parent, Ms. Henderson, said her ideal picture of parent in-volvement in schools was parents monitoring the hallways, the lunch-room, playgrounds, and ultimately working alongside teachers in the classrooms. She just didn't feel like school staff would extend that type of outreach to parents.

Ms. Ingo had a preschooler, kindergartner, and fourth grader. She felt that new teachers were not as friendly and helpful to parents as they needed to be, and their actions kept many parents out of the school. She said the new teachers often kept to themselves, and would be helpful if they reached out to parents more.

Indeed, effective outreach by teachers would likely raise the comfort level of parents. It did for Miranda, once an uninvolved parent, who became very active in her children's education, and in the school. Burton and colleagues (2004) describe Miranda's situation:

> Miranda was a working class African American mother who was rais-ing her two children on her own. She had always wanted her children to succeed in school, but believed she lacked the knowledge, skills, and network of resources to know how to enter into the kinds of activities that made a difference in school. She described her own schooling ex-periences with trepidation—she was a slow learner and never found schools to be a welcoming place. Miranda eventually began to partici-pate in her children's school through a venue created by the caring and

perseverance of her son's teacher. (Burton, Drake, Perez, St. Louis, and George 2004)

CRISIS MODE

Perhaps the greatest obstacle for parent involvement in inner-city schools is what one parent described as "being in crisis mode." She was talking about societal pressures, such as single parenthood, unemployment, low-wage employment, homelessness, substance abuse, domestic violence, unstable or unsafe living conditions, and other issues that may affect an inner-city parent's ability to really focus on their child's school and education.

Bloom (2001) discusses the high expectations schools have for mothers, who are expected to attend parent–teacher conference night, to respond to notes sent home by the school, to chaperone field trips, to volunteer in classrooms, to provide treats for birthday parties, and to run or contribute to fundraisers. It is difficult to imagine a parent who is facing homelessness and hunger being able to seriously focus on getting to a parent–teacher conference or chaperoning a field trip.

Bloom alludes to the contention that expectations, largely middle-class norms, do not apply in inner-city school settings. Bloom writes, "Mothers in poverty, lacking one or more important resources—such as academic skills, emotional well-being, positive ties to schools, a sense of entitlement to be involved in schools, flexible schedules, and money—may find involvement extremely burdensome and psychologically taxing" (2001, 302).

More often than not, being in crisis mode involves grappling with multiple issues. For example, a mother with school-aged children who finds herself and her family hungry, penniless, and homeless as a result of domestic violence may have a difficult time focusing on attending the next PTO meeting, scheduling a parent–teacher conference, or volunteering in her child's classroom.

Ms. Thompson, a parent coordinator at an urban school, talked about the large numbers of families who ate at local shelters every day. She was concerned about whether or not some of the children in the school were actually eating at all in the evenings or on the weekends. For many students, she said, their only meals were the ones eaten in school.

Ms. Thompson was so concerned about the hunger situation among her school families that she considered starting a food pantry at the school. Feedback about the pantry from parents was mixed; some liked the idea, but others felt they would be embarrassed to get food from the school.

Ms. Thompson said many parents told her they were having difficulties paying utility bills. She recalled in several cases referring parents to local social service agencies that provided emergency assistance in the form of money, food, and housing. She was also knowledgeable about payment plans and programs the local utility company administered to help people more easily pay their gas and electric bills.

As a result of economic conditions now, there are many homeless families. Parents raising their families in shelters are much more preoccupied with addressing their current situation, or trying to improve their situation so they can transition into permanent housing. Some shelters have transitional housing programs, along with other counseling services to help the parents get and keep their children in school.

REFLECTIONS

The barriers discussed in this chapter can impede the parent involvement process in education. These barriers are more prevalent in inner-city school environments than in middle-class and suburban school environments. Educators who struggle with parent involvement in inner-city schools may be putting up barriers that are driving parents away. Identifying barriers and eliminating or minimizing them is an important strategy in effectively engaging parents.

FIVE

What to Understand When Engaging Inner-City School Parents

Achieving parent involvement requires hard work. Promoting, implementing, sustaining, expanding, and evaluating parent involvement initiatives requires time, concentration, persistence, energy, research, and passion. Developing parent involvement is like an art. It does not just happen. Someone has to gather the information, survey the circumstances, plan and implement the proper marketing, make the plans, follow up on the details, host the event, and analyze and evaluate the results.

In this chapter we examine the various ways in which educators can solicit and obtain parental involvement within an urban environment and not let it just be an afterthought. Often, outreach activities in some schools that are located in urban environments really seem more like they are fulfilling a necessary requirement than actually trying to engage parents. Parent involvement activities in some schools appear to be put together at the last minute by someone whose job title is anything but parent coordinator, and who may be overwhelmed with responsibilities in the position they were hired to perform.

Extensive preparation must be done if schools intend to be consistently successful in engaging parents. Successfully reaching parents in inner-city schools requires some knowledge and understanding of the characteristics of urban school environments.

TELEPHONES AND COMMUNICATION WITH PARENTS

In today's society where mobile phones are plentiful, the expectation is that educators can pick up the telephone and call parents. Presumably,

59

every parent is easily assessable by phone. However, many parents still do not have access to a phone.

It is not uncommon for inner-city children to come from homes without telephones. A teacher at an inner-city elementary school said that less than one half of the children in her class had telephones, so parents were difficult to reach. Another teacher said that some of her students live in apartment buildings or two- or four-family homes where only one household has a telephone. If a call is made to a parent in that building, the person who has the telephone takes the message and gives it to the parent living in the household with no phone, who calls the school back.

Some administrators in inner-city schools say that they call a lot of phones that are disconnected. This can present serious difficulties for educators and administrators who need to reach parents regarding their children. The telephone, whether it be a cell phone or a home phone, is a fixed expense that many forego in favor of other staples such as housing or food. Some use a prepaid cell phone because they can control the costs. If they do not have the money to add minutes, they do not have a telephone.

Probably the most important situation regarding communication centers on medical conditions involving children. The school nurse is a service provider who frequently interacts with parents and students. The nurse should be able to reach the parents of children who have critical health issues immediately or at least be able to leave a message.

Ms. Roman, a school nurse, said she would see a minimum of twenty students per day for assorted reasons: cuts, bruises, aches and pains, colds and flu, slips, trips, and falls. Some of the common more serious conditions she treated children for were asthma and diabetes, conditions very prevalent among children in inner-city schools. Ms. Roman said that inability to reach parents by phone could have potentially serious consequences. She recalled incidents where children suffering from serious conditions such as asthma had to be transported to the hospital. If the hospital staff can't reach the parents, they are required to get two doctors to consent to prescribe potentially life-saving medications to a sick child.

Whenever Ms. Roman sees a child, she calls his or her parents, even if the visit was minor, just to let the parent know she has seen the child. According to Ms. Roman, many of the children have been taught not to give out their phone numbers. Many families move and change their numbers. Many parents have cell phones, as they are relatively easy to obtain. However, Ms. Roman spoke of the frequent inability to reach parents who had cell phones because the phone was disconnected, the voicemail box was full, there were no minutes left, or the phone was out of range. In cases in which the phone belonged to a neighbor, she felt very uncomfortable leaving a message with a stranger who would then pass the message to the parent when she knew a child was sick.

She believed many inner-city parents have different value systems when it comes to providing contact information. They are not trusting of school staff with their information, or are concerned that their contact information will be shared with people such as bill collectors, law enforcement agencies, and noncustodial parents, to name a few.

Often, inner-city parents do not understand why schools need the correct information. Many parents do not return the emergency contact information card that schools give out at the beginning of the school year or when a new student enrolls in the school. Ms. Roman recalled several incidents where children who were sick or hurt came to see her and she could not reach their parents because the number the school was given had changed or was not in service.

Field trips make having up-to-date contact information vital. The third graders of one inner-city school spent a day at the zoo. One of the children fell and broke his arm. The school had a disconnected phone number for his contact, so the hospital did not have current information. The child did not have a phone number where he could reach his mother. Ultimately, the school social worker went to the child's home to inform the mother that her child had an accident at the zoo.

Most principals regret when they cannot let a child go on a field trip because their parents did not sign a permission slip. The challenges start, of course, with the disappointment on the child's face when the child realizes he or she cannot go on the trip with the rest of the class. Situations like these are problematic because the school has to plan for proper supervision and instruction for the child or children who cannot go on the field trip.

Ms. Roman, the school nurse, was very concerned about children who were either on medication or whom she thought could benefit from being on medication. She recalled children suffering from attention-deficit/hyperactivity disorder (ADHD) who perhaps had run out of medication or were not on medication and were transported from the school to the emergency room when their behavior became uncontrollable or violent. If school officials could not reach the parents, two doctors in the emergency room were required to agree to sign off on the action to prescribe thirty days' worth of ADHD medication and require parents to take their child to a doctor for a follow up visit. According to Ms. Roman, often parents do not follow up with the recommended doctor visits, and children do not receive additional medication after the thirty-day supply is depleted.

Ms. Roman was also concerned about immunizations. Schools should not admit children who have not had proper immunizations, but many schools admit the students anyway. She explained that the district conducted an audit early in the school year for grades kindergarten and seven as well as for those students new to the district. The most recent audit at her school showed that only 21.4 percent of the children were in compliance. In that district, the school was expected to be at 93-percent compliance by the end of the school year.

Ms. Roman recalled "Exclusion Day," which occurs in late fall, when students without proof of proper immunizations are sent home. By the time Exclusion Day occurs, the school has sent out at least five notices warning the parent that the child needs to be immunized. Of these five notices, three are sent home with the student and two are sent via U.S. mail. One school had about forty students affected by Exclusion Day. The office was packed with children being sent home who were waiting on their parents.

Ms. Roman fondly recalled one parent who is an employee at one of the local hospitals who received the phone call to pick up her son who was not properly immunized. She was very embarrassed and immediately picked up her child and took him to one of the neighborhood clinics for his immunizations. They were back at the school in about twenty minutes. The mother advised that her son admitted that he never gave her the forms when they were sent home, and had intercepted the ones sent via U.S. mail. As a result, she made her son pay the $.50 fee that the clinic charged to conduct the immunizations with proceeds from his part-time job.

Ms. Roman talked about how frustrating it is to get parents to respond to certain requests. She had fifty students who, through a free eye exam administered by LensCrafters, were diagnosed as needing eyeglasses. Parents only needed to sign the form authorizing the fitting of free glasses for the students and return it to the school. By the deadline, she had received no signed forms. The school sent the forms home with the students and mailed them to the parents. She also gave forms to parents she saw in the building. Eventually, she conducted home visits to get most of the forms signed.

FORMS

Forms are perceived by some as a middle-class phenomenon. They seem to multiply and get more and more complicated. While forms seem to be a necessary evil, they just do not get the same kind of attention from parents in inner-city schools. Ms. Thompson, the community resource coordinator at an inner-city school, said that about 150 students qualified for free tutoring under the No Child Left Behind Act. To get the free tutoring, parents had to complete a form and return it to the school. By the deadline, only 20 of the 150 parents had returned the forms.

The form itself was complicated. It was two pages long with very small print and a lot of confusing educational jargon. One parent admitted she felt intimidated by the form. Another parent said he could not read very well and had trouble completing the form, so he said, "Forget it."

A missing or nonupdated form, such as the emergency contact forms many schools require, hinders schools from being able to give parents important updates or announcements. An incorrect or missing address or phone number may cause parents to not receive information about an upcoming school event such as a musical or theatrical performance or an open house. When a teacher wants to give a parent good news about a child's academic performance, he or she cannot deliver the news by phone or mail without contact information.

Even report cards that are sent home for the parents' signatures are often not returned. One teacher of a class of fourteen students sent report cards home four times per year with the expectation that they would be signed and returned; two signed report cards were returned the entire year. The exception occurred during the quarter that the school decided to require that parents come to the school to retrieve their children's cards. Then nine of the fourteen parents came to school to sign the cards.

One inner-city school in a large Midwestern city held quarterly events where they would serve food and have activities and guest speakers for the entire family. These events would yield over two hundred to three hundred parents along with their children. All teachers were required to attend and be ready to hand out report cards and discuss them with the parents. One of the quarterly events took place in February during a snowstorm where most of the city was closed because of weather. Despite the storm, over eight hundred parents and students showed up for the event.

However, another inner-city school in the same town held an evening open house, where no food or activities were provided, but parents were asked to come to the school to pick up their child's report card. Although the school had about four hundred students, only thirty parents came to retrieve the report cards.

There were many sick children at one inner-city school in a large Midwestern city. Per Ms. Moore, the school social worker, the majority of the children had no medical insurance coverage. She said that most would be eligible for free health insurance from the government but parents did not apply for the coverage. She said many had no reportable income or were possibly paid in cash. Some parents worked, for example, in bars or small diners, braided hair in their homes, or cleaned people's houses, and were paid in cash. They felt uncomfortable filling out a form that required them to report their income.

A similar situation occurs with the form parents must complete for their children to receive free lunch. At one school, the lunchroom staff took a hardline stance about not giving free lunch to students who did not have a form on file. Many students went hungry that day because the staff refused to serve children whose parents had not completed the form. Outraged, teachers went out and bought peanut butter and jelly and bread and made sandwiches for the hungry children, many of whom possibly would not get a meal that day except at school. The principal ultimately overruled the lunchroom staff's decision and allowed all children to eat, regardless of whether or not a form was on file.

PARENTS AND TECHNOLOGY

Even though the cost of home computers has decreased significantly over the last couple of decades, many families in low-income communities do not consider them an affordable expense. Even if a family has a computer, maintenance and upkeep can be a substantial cost that could leave it inoperable, and some cannot afford the expense of Internet access.

Still many parents in low-income communities are now finding ways to access computers on a daily basis. Some are fortunate to have jobs where they can access the computer at work. One parent of a small child in a Midwestern inner-city neighborhood elected to go back to college in an online program. She did not have a computer at home, so she was doing her homework by hand and accessing her computer at work over her lunch period, and for the few minutes before and after work that she had time to do it. Over a period of several months, she was able to save enough money to get a computer for about $400 from Walmart.

Parents without computers in the house can also find them in public libraries. Most libraries have a limited number of computers that can be utilized with a valid library card for a set period of time, say ninety minutes. Parents in college can also utilize computer labs on campus.

Many school systems now provide access to student progress online. In one Midwestern school district, teachers enter data such as homework assignments, assignments missed, test scores, and attendance. One single father of a student in one of the inner-city high schools used the system to track his daughter's progress on a regular basis. "I am able to see her homework assignments and grades, and even busted her skipping school once because of the attendance screen," he said.

PARENT–TEACHER CONFERENCES

Parent–teacher conferences provide a great opportunity for outreach between parents and teachers. Parents get to see their children's work and discuss ways they can help them succeed. If properly engaged by the teacher, parents can provide unique insights into the child's background and interests.

Several principals said they have challenges getting parents to come to parent–teacher conferences. Many teachers will make phone calls to as many parents as possible, but they still do not show for the conferences.

Most teachers will say that usually the same few parents diligently show up for conferences. Teachers often regret never meeting some of the parents of the children that they have grown fond of. They regret that they cannot meet, discuss, and maybe strategize with the parents of students with serious academic and or behavior problems.

Lack of parent participation in parent–teacher conferences is unfortunate. Often parents can provide information about their children that is not apparent to teachers. One parent who attended a conference with her daughter's second grade teacher was told that it was unfortunate that the little girl could not read. The mother was astonished to hear that because her daughter had participated in Head Start since she was three and actually could read. After communicating this to the teacher, the next day the teacher interacted with the student and find out that she could indeed read at a higher level than second grade. The girl was just very shy and was afraid to speak when called on to read out loud.

Another teacher found out from a parent–teacher conference at an inner-city school in a large Midwestern city that one of her students had been taking piano lessons and at age eleven was an accomplished pianist. The next time the school had an assembly the child was given a chance to play and showcase his talent to the entire school.

Mr. Duncan, a middle school teacher, said that parents of about eight of the ninety middle school students attended conferences. He saw the mother of one of his behaviorally challenged students at the school one day and she told him she received the notices for conferences, but never attended because she had other things to do. One parent with a fourth grade daughter who only recently started attending conferences admitted that for her it was a generational thing because her mother never came to the school. "If your parents never came to parent–teacher conferences, you won't either," she said.

Ms. Andrews, a former middle school teacher in a large Southeastern inner-city school, said that parents of her twenty to twenty-five students per class rarely showed for conferences. "I felt like the ones that showed usually wanted to fuss about something," she said. "One parent showed up because her daughter got an F. I was glad she showed up because I was able to show her where her daughter missed all the words on the spelling test. Regretfully, the parent said it was my fault and that I was a bad teacher."

Although Ms. Andrews was really hurt by the exchange, she remembered telling the parent she was sorry the parent felt that way, and that she would work harder to help the child. "She actually became one of my better students," she said.

CRISIS MODE

Many parents are in crisis mode. Because the majority of the children come from low-income families, they may be struggling with staples that others take for granted, such as food and clothing.

Ms. Moore said that she solicited many local businesses and organizations for donations for students and their families. For the holidays one year, she collected seven hundred hat and glove sets, two hundred and fifty department store certificates, one hundred grocery store certificates, many sets of underwear and socks, and a large amount of hygiene products. She distributed all the items at a holiday party at the school.

Homelessness also plagues families in inner cities. Some families travel from home to home or from shelter to shelter. Family mobility can affect the school's ability to reach the parent, and the lack of stability can easily affect a child's ability to learn.

One mother and her child had to leave their apartment immediately because the building had some environmental hazards that caused the building to be condemned. They spent several nights with relatives before they were able to get into another apartment.

Other families are finding their lives disrupted by the bed bug epidemic. One family in a Midwestern inner city was directed by the landlord to remove their mattress, their clothing, and their couch and chairs from the building and put them in a dumpster he rented. So in a matter of minutes, a family of four had no clothes and no beds to sleep on.

Ms. Andrews remembered a child in her class named Linda. One day Linda's mother came to the classroom after class and told her that she had just been evicted from their apartment and asked if she and Linda could stay a few days with Ms. Andrews. "I felt bad because I had to tell her no, although I was kind of happy that she felt comfortable enough with me as her daughter's teacher to confide in me," she said. "I gave her some information on shelters she could go to and after that, I never saw either of them again." Presumably, Linda had to enroll in a school in another community.

Another very sad situation Ms. Andrews remembered was that of a academically high-achieving student who lived on the street with her mother. Her mother was very ill with lupus, and they literally lived on the street, but the child always managed to get her homework done.

YOUNG PARENTS

The schools are full of young children with very young parents, some in their teens and early twenties. One principal talked about kindergarteners who had eighteen- or nineteen-year-old parents whom she had taught just a few years back. Principals, teachers, and other school professionals express that many parents, particularly the younger ones, utilize the school as a daycare center, although the merits of that comment are debatable. It is a relative concept. Any busy parent would rather have his or her child in school than home alone, and the fact is, regardless of how parents plan to spend their day, they are allowed and are expected to have their children in school during the day.

Around 750,000 teens in the United States between fifteen and nineteen become pregnant every year. Many live in inner cities in poverty. Many of these teen mothers are living at home with their parents in poverty, or with a single parent who helps them care for their child or children. Studies show that children who live in poverty tend to have children who continue to live in poverty, and that single parents tend to have children who become single parents. While there are many wonderful examples of children who overcame poor backgrounds and went on to achieve great accomplishments, and children of single parents going on to become happily married members of society, most teen mothers are part of a continuing cycle of poverty and single parenthood that continues generation after generation.

Mr. Duncan, a middle school teacher, felt the lack of sustained parent involvement at his school was related to the age of parents, many of whom were not ready to become parents. "There are lots of young parents here—mid 20s, multiple kids," he said. "Many young parents are no more ready for parenthood than the man in the moon."

ANGRY PARENTS

Some parents come into the school irate and ready to yell at the staff. While parents wielding weapons should be subdued, reported to the police, or asked to leave, depending on the circumstances, it is probably better to let upset parents vent. More often than not, they just really want to be heard.

Parents can get emotional about their children. It is natural for a parent to support his or her child, at least until the parent has the whole story. Some parents have come to the school irate because their child was suspended or expelled, and the parents ended up being arrested. Some school districts issue "stay away letters" to parents who are loud, irate, or violent. Certainly, in situations of assault or violence against school staff, such an action may be appropriate, but more often than not, letting parents be heard could resolve a situation.

Ms. Hamilton, a parent of a fourth grader in an inner-city school in a Midwestern city, believes that being in crisis mode might contribute to a parent's erratic behavior. She has seen parents yell at teachers. "You ain't gonna do this to my child," she mimicked. "Sometimes yelling at the teacher may make them feel better about their situation," she said. Ms.

Hamilton believes teachers need to develop better coping skills and patience when dealing with parents of children in inner-city schools. "They just don't know what kinds of challenges parents went through before they came into that school," she said.

Ms. Johnson came to school mad at everyone in sight. She felt her daughter was being bullied and felt the teachers were letting it happen. She came into the school office demanding in a loud voice to speak to the principal, who ultimately came out of a meeting in his office to calm her down. Once she got a chance to voice her concerns, she and the principal were able to come to resolution regarding her daughter.

Sometimes angry parents are cynical about the school's ability to education their children. One parent remembered being very angry when she noticed that her daughter never seemed to get any homework, yet her daughter could barely read. She went to the school, yelling through the halls as she went, demanding to talk to the teacher in the middle of the day. The teacher, who appeared scared by her presence, called the office, and the school security guard came to the room and escorted the irate parent to the principal's office, where she demanded answers. The principal was able to facilitate a meeting between the parent and the teacher, who agreed to give more individualized attention to her daughter.

Mr. Duncan, who had been teaching in middle school for over ten years, acknowledged that his school had many new, less experienced teachers who were not used to the inner-city school environment. "Everyone doesn't understand inner-city kids. Mom is on crack; Dad is in prison; brother on the corner selling dope. That's the environment many of these students come from," he said.

He said that many of the new teachers were scared of irate parents, and were usually quick to call him or the principal than deal with them. "Sometimes you have to just let them vent and then they calm down and go on about their business," he said. "It's only when they won't go away, or when they appear to be under the influence of something, or look like they want to get physical that I call the principal for help."

PARENTS WHO HAVE NOT BEEN INVOLVED

As indicated in chapter 3, a number of parental situations in the inner-city school may or may not be present in a suburban school. Some parents have been in prison. One principal talked about discussions he had with a mother recently released from prison, having served eight years, and who had just regained custody of her sons and was going through an adjustment period. He said the adjustment was also difficult for the boys, who were used to not having a mother around, and were having some behavioral problems in school. He also talked about a few fathers he was counseling because they had been in jail, or had just been absentee parents for years, and who wanted his help in making the transition back into their children's lives easier.

Some parents work multiple jobs or go to school full-time and leave their children with a relative such as a grandparent most of the time. They may not have the time or the energy to spend much time in their children's schools. One mom talked about how she worked two jobs so she would pick up her son and daughter at 9 p.m. at her mother's house on a weeknight. She really depended on her mother to make sure her children ate dinner and did their homework.

Some people have no particular barriers that hinder them from being involved. If their own parents were not involved in their educational experiences for whatever reason, they did not learn to be involved. Some parents feel that once their children get to school, it is the responsibility of the school to educate them, and they are absolved of any accountability for their learning. Some parents do not know the value of parent involvement to the education of their children, or may not believe that they can really have a positive impact on the academic development of their children.

SUBSTANCE ABUSE

Parents with substance abuse issues are present in all schools. However, they seem to be prevalent in some inner-city schools. Many inner-city school parents need help on various levels. One principal estimated that about 60 percent of the parents he met suffered from some kind of substance abuse issue. Many urban schools are located in areas fraught with drug dealers and stores and nightclubs that sell liquor. Getting high or intoxicated is relatively easy in that neighborhood. However, nightclubs have a strong influence in some inner-city communities. For some people, employment at a nightclub represents a means of income, a means of keeping food on the table and providing shelter. For others, the club may represent a necessary outlet to vent their frustrations.

As indicated, the nurse said some parents would talk freely about their own drug and alcohol abuse problems. Teachers spoke of parents that sometimes would come into the school who appeared to be under the influence of something, and some school staff indicated they could smell liquor on the breath of some parents. This is a real dilemma in some inner-city schools located in neighborhoods where drugs, bars, and liquor stores are readily available. One inner-city school was involved in the development of a partnership with a local health clinic to provide free counseling for parents who were substance abusers.

NEIGHBORHOOD SURROUNDINGS

The neighborhood surroundings of an inner-city school are different from middle-class environments. Students may be able to see drug dealers, pimps, and prostitutes from the windows of the school building. They walk past them on the way to and from school.

Urban neighborhoods are full of young men, often school dropouts hanging on the streets. Many are involved in drug dealing. They make their "living" selling drugs.

Succumbing to the harshness of poverty and crime, many young men in the inner city are involved with gangs. They look to gang-related activity for companionship, financial support, self-esteem, and protection.

Violent crime is ever-present in the inner city. Drive-by shootings occur on a regular basis. Often the intended target of the violence is shot, which is sad, but what is really sad is when innocent bystanders get hurt or killed by gunfire. A grandmother waiting at a bus stop within a few blocks of a school in a Midwestern urban city was killed by a stray bullet. On another day, two children walking home from a nearby elementary school stopped at the store and were both hit by stray bullets from a drive-by shooting. Fortunately, their wounds were not serious.

Other senseless shootings claim random victims in inner-city environments. A man sitting in a crowded bar in the inner city of a Midwestern city was killed by a bullet intended for someone else. A teenager was paralyzed from the chest down by a stray bullet as she was eating at a local restaurant in the inner core of the same city. A few miles away, a teenager was killed by a bullet intended for someone else as he attended a party.

Theft is still prevalent in the inner city. A woman in an inner-city housing project in a Southern city left her purse on the front seat of her car for about two minutes while she went to pick up something from a friend. The front passenger side window was about three-quarters rolled up. When she came back to her car, her purse was gone. A woman in a Midwestern inner-city neighborhood parked her car outside a job training center while she spent about three hours in training. When she returned to her car, the rear driver's side window was broken and her daughter's book bag, which was in the back seat, was gone.

People get held up at gunpoint and knifepoint for money, jewelry, watches, cell phones, and other personal items. One man recently spoke of a man on an inner-city street who showed him a gun and demanded his wallet. Fearful for his safety, he gave it to him.

Many neighborhoods around schools in the urban core are fraught with litter. The array of litter found in these neighborhoods is diverse. Cigarette butts, fast food bags, food wrappers, pop cans, and liquor bottles are just examples of the kinds of litter in the streets. One early morning, a teacher found a used needle on the steps of a school in a Midwestern city. Overnight, someone had been on the school grounds shooting up drugs. Luckily, she was the first to arrive at the school that day as opposed to a young child who may have picked up the needle, curious as to what it was.

There are many vacant buildings in inner-city neighborhoods across the country. Often the buildings are unkempt. Vacant buildings tend to attract illegal activity. Drug use, prostitution, and even homeless squatters with no place to go end up in empty buildings. In one Midwestern city, squatters living in a vacant house started a fire trying to keep warm. Shortly, the entire house was in flames, rendering the structure a total loss, and yet another eyesore to an already dilapidated neighborhood.

Many inner-city neighborhoods have little green space. Green space is aesthetically pleasing, and depending on how it is structured, can provide play space for children. Most children in inner-city neighborhoods across the country have to travel outside their neighborhoods to find appropriate green space for recreation that suburban children take for granted.

As middle-class and White residents move out of the urban core, so do much of the business and industry. Many inner cities have no banks, grocery stores, pharmacies, or retail shopping opportunities. Some urban families take one or two buses to areas out of the neighborhood to get the basic necessities that others easily get. Or they buy necessities at exorbitant costs at the few corner stores left. Some discount or "dollar" stores exist in inner cities, but certain items such as fresh fruit and vegetables and prescriptions are difficult to find in many urban areas.

Many businesses that were formerly located in the inner city have relocated out of the urban core and into suburban communities that may provide amenities such as more space, better parking options for employees and customers, a safer working environment, or more positive tax consequences. Empty warehouses and buildings in inner-city communities across the country are creating eyesores, taking up space that could be better utilized, and providing breeding grounds for criminal activity.

Businesses that employ inner-city residents who move out of urban areas have a devastating effort on those environments. Depending on where they relocate, residents may have transportation challenges trying to get to work, and if they move to areas not easily accessible by public transportation, people who do not have cars may have problems getting to work and may have to quit or they may lose their jobs.

Depending on an area's tax structure, if a business that employs multiple people moves out of a city, any payroll taxes paid to the city move with it. A city may lose income via property taxes if a business moves out of the area. Any retail or service establishments or other businesses that depend on employees from a large company in the area can be financially affected, such as restaurants, stores, or dry cleaners, for example.

REFLECTIONS

Inner-city school educators and administrators who understand that their job is not just about understanding curriculum and instruction are the most successful. Inner-city school administrators and teachers have to learn what factors influence the parent-outreach process, and they have to understand how to deal with parents or circumvent them to overcome the challenges associated with educating their students.

Working in inner-city school environments requires another level of learning for the educator beyond the basics of teaching and administration mastered in higher education institutions. Many educators don't learn that until they actually get into the inner-city schoolhouse fraught with all its unique concerns. To be successful with parent outreach in inner-city schools, educators must seek to become aware of social and economic issues that might stifle the expected academic process and learn how to address those issues to the benefit of the student.

SIX

Alternative Schools and Urban America

Long gone are the days when the traditional inner-city school is the only option for parents and children living in urban America. So many urban schools are considered failing and thus parents do not have to settle for the nearest public school anymore. Cities are filled with tuition-free charter schools and private schools, some which offer generous scholarships to attract inner-city youth. In addition, more and more inner-city youth are being homeschooled. Furthermore, many parents, frustrated with the academic performance of their neighborhood schools, the level of attention given to the needs of their child or children, or the treatment given to them as parents, have begun to exercise their right of "school choice" and enroll their children in one of thousands of public-supported charter schools. This chapter examines these trends and some of the implications of the movement away from the more traditional public schools.

A charter school operates based on a contract between the school and another entity. In some areas that entity is a local school district. In others it may be the state department of education or oversight agency. States differ in what types of organizations or groups can operate charter schools. Nonprofit organizations, for-profit entities, postsecondary institutions, teacher or parent groups, or private corporations are examples of entities that operate charter schools across the country. Charter schools usually have boards of directors that provide leadership by setting policy, conducting strategic planning, and monitoring and sustaining the overall financial stability of the organization.

Charter schools contract between the school and the sponsor to determine the rules of operation, but generally they do not have the level of bureaucracy present in most urban public school systems. They do not have unions, so the administrators have greater autonomy with directing the teachers who do not have limited hours per day that they can work; in contrast, some traditional school districts have policies that a teacher can work no longer than, say, eight hours per day. Charter schools often do not limit the length of a school day or week. Subsequently, many charter schools offer regular Saturday school. Charter schools have greater control over personnel expenses, so teacher and staff salaries and benefits may not be to the level of those at traditional public school systems, or they may be higher.

Urban charter schools are often started as a result of a movement to provide something that is missing or that is perceived to be missing in the traditional school system. For example, some charter schools have themes of interest to parents seeking better opportunities for their children. Possible themes are college preparatory, math and science, leadership, special needs, foreign language, and the arts.

Some charter schools deliberately direct their recruiting efforts toward the toughest at-risk students. One charter high school in an urban Midwestern environment purposefully recruits children who have failed at other schools. The school keeps its enrollment at two hundred students or fewer to be able to provide unlimited special attention to each student to ensure success. They see parents as partners in the process and welcome their involvement in the classroom, at parent–teacher conferences, and at school-sponsored events.

Many inner-city charter schools have the same trouble as traditional public schools attracting and utilizing parents. One urban charter school has been a high performing school academically, but its success is largely attributed to having a ten-hour day during which the school serves a complete breakfast and lunch, students spend the entire day learning, and the teachers are not part of a union that limits the amount of time they can spend at work. Teachers spend as much time as needed to support the student, and as a result, this school is among the highest performing schools in the city, and definitely among the most successful charter schools.

One urban charter school had a small parent group of about ten parents. The school had five hundred students. The ten parents that consistently showed up were interested and enthusiastic, but lacked the experience to really organize, and unfortunately, the school had limited resources in the way of teachers or administrators to help them get organized. There was no parent coordinator in the school. The parents talked about having a fundraiser, but the principal told them what was really needed was someone to assist with state standardized tests for the many students who had individualized education plans (IEPs) and required someone to read the test to them. A few of the parents confessed that they did not read well and were not comfortable in participating in such a role.

Private schools are owned and operated by a nongovernment entity. Most if not all of their funding comes from private individuals, interest groups, organizations, or corporations. Private schools usually charge tuition, and can be selective in terms of the students they accept. They can also have more liberal dismissal or expulsion policies than public schools. Like charter schools, they usually have a board that provides overall leadership and strategic planning for the institution.

Private schools often have a parent involvement requirement. These requirements can range from a commitment to a minimum number of volunteer hours to a significant time commitment to certain initiatives, such as attendance at parent–teacher conferences or regular parent meetings. Some schools require parents to assist with activities such as fundraisers, field trips, or special after-school programs.

Avon Academy is a small private school in an urban area. Most of the students are African Americans from low- and middle-income families. The school is very small; only about three hundred students attend from grades kindergarten through eight. Many families can hardly afford to pay the tuition and receive some financial assistance through an endowment from the school. The entire school consists of a few small buildings nestled in a small, park-like settling at the dead end of a city street.

Classes at Avon are small, with no more than ten students in a room. Students receive highly individualized attention; many of the graduates are qualified to go on to some of the best high school college preparatory programs.

The school has a parent involvement contract that must be adhered to. Parents are required to give ten hours per school year to volunteer activities for the school. The school is very organized and deliberate about the kinds of activities parents are to be involved in. Examples are lunch duty, field trips, program activities, parent–teacher organization, hall monitoring, and volunteering in the classroom. Parents who do not participate are admonished and threatened with dismissal of their children from school.

Kim had one daughter at Avon named Keisha. Her daughter really thrived in the small class setting. The individualized attention enabled Keisha to excel beyond her years academically. Her state standardized test scores were always well above the national average. She excelled in math, and was able to transition into one of the top high schools in the city. Kim felt consistent parent involvement in the school was a contributing factor in the success of the school, and of her daughter. "We [the parents] did a little bit of everything," she said.

> We worked in the classroom helping the teacher. We monitored the halls during changing of classes. We tutored kids. We helped clean up rooms after school. I organized and worked on some of the fundraisers [candy sales]. Because we participated, the teachers had more time to

spend on teaching. And it was so helpful that we didn't have to guess about how we could help; they carefully took the time to decide where they could use us and teachers were appreciative of our help and didn't make us feel like outsiders. I also think that for my daughter, seeing me so active in school gave her extra incentive to do well herself.

Parochial schools offer a private school option for inner-city parents who want to ensure a strong education for their children. Parochial schools are private schools that are operated and supported by a religious organization. The Catholic faith probably operates the most parochial schools nationwide, although schools operated by other religious denominations are growing in popularity. Often inner-city students are not necessarily members of the religion backing the school, but parents are satisfied with the level of academic excellence associated with the school.

Most parochial schools have a parent-involvement expectation. They often have stated parameters within a contract parents sign at the time of enrollment. Some schools have family volunteer requirements, which include children or even extended family. Some have different requirements for single-parent families.

Saint Stephens, located in the inner center of a large Midwestern city, requires each family to volunteer only one hour per month, but one hour per month for nine months multiplied by three hundred families equals 3,600 volunteer hours per school year, which is significant. Most urban public schools could never boast such hours.

Faith sent her third grade daughter, Alisha, to a Catholic school. The school did not have a specific requirement for volunteer hours for parents, but parents were required to attend quarterly conferences with the teachers. "They accepted no excuses for [not] attending the scheduled conferences. They tried to be flexible with times if I had to work, but I had to make those conferences as a part of her being there," she said. "Sometimes I took vacation days to make sure I could be there."

Faith was impressed by the organization of the conferences. "The teacher would show me all her work, and any problems she had, as well as improvements," she said. "They also gave me ideas on what I could do to help—ways I could help her do better. Not hard things, just like asking her about her homework, and having her read things to me and show me things."

Homeschooling is the ultimate experience in parent involvement. Parents are totally involved in the process from start to finish. They choose the curriculum, the teaching methods, and the process of assessment of learning. Some homeschooling does exist in the inner city, often influenced by a parent's frustration involving lack of adequate attention to their children in their traditional public school, safety issues, religious concerns, or frustration with teachers or administrators in the public school.

Debra homeschooled her three children because she was dissatisfied with the level of safety in the public schools and felt that the teachers she'd encountered were ineffective with her children. They lived in the urban core of a large Midwestern city. Debra was a single parent, widowed a number of years earlier, who worked at a local nonprofit within walking distance from her home. All three of her children, Todd, 16, Nia, 13, and Mark, 10, had been to regular public schools with average academic success. All three of her children are intelligent children, and all are taller than average for their age, but Todd was also a little heavy. Unlike other children his size, he was shy and often picked on by bullies. Debra would often get calls from the high school that Todd was involved in fights. But the events of one day convinced her that public school would no longer work for Todd.

Debra got a call from the school that Todd had been in a fight again. She left work immediately and went to the school and found Todd sitting in a chair in the hall doing nothing. When she asked the teacher why her child was sitting outside in the hall, the teacher said she asked Todd what happened when she heard a disturbance in the back of the room and he would not say anything so she felt he was being defiant and she made him sit out in the hall.

Debra was infuriated that Todd was being "punished" and the other children involved were in class absorbing the lesson, which is what she wanted for her child. She believed that because Todd was tall and heavy, the short, young, petite white female teacher, who was in her first year of teaching, was intimidated by him and thought the easiest way to deal with him was to set him out in the hall. Debra complained to the principal about the situation. However, the principal gave her a general response that he supported the teachers in their efforts to discipline students. So that was when she made the bold decision to homeschool Todd.

She went to the public school district office and obtained a packet that they provided to homeschool parents. Most school districts provide some support to local homeschool parents, realizing that they are taxpayers and are entitled to such services. She was able to get free textbooks from the school district (although they were usually not the latest edition), and she got help from friends and co-workers who worked one-on-one with Todd on subjects he had challenges with. After a few months, she decided to homeschool all three children together.

All three children and Debra would get up early in the morning and Debra would work with them for a few hours before she left for work. They had work plans that they had to fulfill daily, and Debra would check their progress at the end of each day. Although the commitment to homeschooling her children was a challenge that tested her knowledge, time management, and patience, Debra found that all the stress associated with having to deal with inexperienced, unqualified teachers or nonempathetic administrators was gone because she had firsthand knowledge of her children's issues.

Of course Debra was concerned with how she would develop their socialization skills. She was able to connect locally with other homeschool parents, some in inner-city situations like hers and others in suburban environments, and have the children participate in field trips to museums, the zoo, nature preserves, and other places. At 6'7" Mark was the tallest child and played in a youth basketball league. Todd enjoyed all kinds of art and participated with an art club. Nia was tall and beautiful like a model, so she participated with a modeling club. All three successfully met the requirements for graduation and participated in a special graduation ceremony with other homeschooled children. All three enrolled in college.

Angela was another single parent who decided to homeschool her daughter in the inner center of a large Midwestern city. She was frustrated by the fact that her special-needs daughter, Whitney, who was diagnosed with a learning disability, could not get the services she needed at the local public school. Whitney was a fourth grader who could barely read a sentence. For the preceding three years, Angela had complained that her daughter seemed to be lagging behind the other children. Her complaints went largely ignored. She finally requested that her daughter be evaluated for an IEP and after several months, she was finally given an IEP.

However, Angela felt that the IEP meetings were unproductive and that her opinions about how they could better serve her child were marginalized. "So I made the tough decision to pursue homeschooling with my baby girl. It was a hard decision because I questioned how I could help my child with no training as a teacher and only a high school education myself," she said. "But I figured if I knew enough to get a high school degree, that I should be able to help my daughter get one." Angela recognized that she is the expert on her own child.

Angela was unemployed and contemplating going back to school for a nursing degree. She decided that for the moment, she would put her energy into helping her daughter. "I went to the library and got as much information as I could," she said. "I went to her doctor and got some recommendations on people who could help her with her work, and help me help her." As a result, Whitney is now in the sixth grade and is reading at the sixth-grade level. Angela plans to homeschool her through the eighth grade, and then together they will decide if it is time for her to consider enrolling in a traditional high school. She will also decide then if it is time for her to pursue that nursing degree she always wanted.

Denise was a single mother with four children, a son in seventh grade and a son in sixth grade at a charter school, and a daughter in first grade and another daughter in third grade in a traditional public school. She noticed a difference in the outreach to parents in the charter school as opposed to the traditional public school.

"At my boys' school, they worked with me; they kept in contact with me," she said. "When my boys had a problem, the teacher would immediately call me." Denise was raising her children alone while attending college full-time to earn a bachelor's degree. She had limited time to be involved with her children's schools. "My boys' school was way more accommodating than my girls' school," she said. "I have parent–teacher conferences over the phone with my boys' teachers." Her boys seemed to do better academically than the girls.

Denise cited a lack of communication and a seeming disrespect for the parents as the major problems with the public school the girls attended. "They would let us know a day or two ahead of time that they scheduled a parent–teacher conference for us at a particular time," she said. "Of course I could never make them. They were always at times when I was in school. I'm sure many parents had the same problem. Then they would talk about how nobody showed up for conferences."

The teachers and administrators of Denise's boys' charter school encouraged parents to be in the building. "They [teachers] are excited when parents come in," she said. "Teachers would say, I'm glad you're here." Although Denise could not be at the school on a regular basis, she volunteered there twice per month for a couple of hours at a time, answering phones, serving lunch, and working in a classroom.

Her experience with her girls' traditional school was totally different. She could not attend the scheduled parent–teacher conferences, and would call and leave messages for the teacher with no response. She got no response until her third grade daughter came home with straight Fs on her report card. It was frustrating for her because she felt she was not given an opportunity to help, and only when she went to the principal and insisted that he tell the teacher to meet with her did she get the feedback she needed to help her daughter.

Initially, Denise could only get her two oldest children into the charter school because there were no more vacancies. After a year, she was able to get the girls into the charter school as well, and all four children are doing well academically. The set-up allows her to have more volunteer time at the school because they are all together.

Within urban public school systems are alternatives to the traditional schools. Magnet schools are usually organized around some theme, such as the arts, college preparation, or foreign language, for example. Magnet schools usually produce high-performing students and have high levels of parent participation at school-sponsored events and activities, Parent–Teacher Associations and Organizations, and parent–teacher conferences.

Urban systems interested in producing effective schools with strong parent involvement should consider emulating Debbie Meier. She has shown several times over that a creative approach to learning and embracing parents as partners in education produces excellent results. And she did it in some of the toughest inner-city environments in America.

Debbie Meier founded small alternative schools in Harlem and Boston. Children were not admitted based on ability or anything specific. She employed innovative teaching methods, like using real-life nature to teach science in the park, which appealed to students.

Meier encouraged parent involvement in the education of her students. Communication with parents was a priority. She respected their right and need to know what was happening in the school and what was happening with each child. Parent–teacher meetings were a regular part of the process, where teachers were expected to encourage parent input in their children's learning experiences. As a result of her efforts, most of the students in her school went on to college.

Another example of a successful inner-city school initiative is Harlem Children's Zone, Inc., led by president and chief executive officer Geoffrey Canada. For the last twenty years, Canada has run the Harlem Children's Zone, which provides educational, medical, and social services to children and families in a one hundred–block area in central Harlem.

Parent and family involvement plays a key role in the success of the Harlem Children's Zone. Baby College is a nine-week parenting program. There are asthma and obesity initiatives. The Family Development Program and the Family Support Center are designed to help resolve issues hindering the success of children in school. Canada recognizes the need for strong, healthy families to promote more successful educational experiences for children.

Nontraditional schools are just as much a part of the inner city as traditional schools. Parents see them as filling a need for the children that traditional public schools do not fill. Parent involvement challenges are as much a part of these schools as they are in traditional inner-city schools. However, some schools, such as the religious and private schools, have parent involvement contracts or requirements, which result in many hundreds of hours of valuable volunteer time spent in schools. Parent involvement is the cornerstone of homeschooling, which likely contributes to the success of homeschooled children. Educators in all types of schools value the role of parents in creating successful learning environments.

SEVEN

Parent Involvement and Health Issues

Among the most important issues of concern to parents is the health of their children. Whether parents have children in an urban or suburban school environment, the health and well being of their children are of paramount concern. The health of a child can define his or her livelihood, school experience, and social interactions.

The health of a child is closely tied to his or her performance in school. How a child feels or manages a health challenge may dictate how well he or she masters the school work. That is why parents closely oversee the health of their children. For example, a child in pain may have great difficulty concentrating in school. A child with vision problems may struggle to read a book or see the blackboard. This chapter discusses the nexus between parental involvement and the general health of their children as urban school students. This chapter seeks to examine the link between the health of students and parental involvement.

For example, asthma is a lung disease that obstructs airways and causes breathing problems. Over seven million children in the United States suffer from asthma, many of whom live in the inner city. The very nature of the urban core contributes to the susceptibility of children to asthma. The pollution in cities due to the large influx of automobiles affects the air children breathe, as do the emissions from industrial plants, fumes from toxic waste sites, and increased pollen. Those factors, combined with climatic conditions that exist in certain areas of the country, can increase the incidence of pediatric asthma.

Living conditions can influence a child's likelihood of developing asthma. For example, cigarette smoke in the home may trigger asthma attacks in children. Living near a dump site or an industrial plant can also elicit an asthmatic reaction.

Asthma among children and adults in the inner city has also been associated with cockroaches. In one study of inner-city children, 37 percent were allergic to cockroaches. Frequent hospital admissions of inner-city children often are directly related to their contact with cockroach allergens.

Inner-city children are also susceptible to mouse allergens. Mouse allergens are prevalent in inner-city homes. A study led by Dr. Elizabeth Matsui (2005) at the Johns Hopkins Children's Center collected air and dust samples from the bedrooms of one hundred inner-city children with asthma and found that 84 percent of bedrooms had detectable levels of mouse allergen.

These and other allergies cause more problems if the school has an infestation. Inner-city schools that are unkempt should be of great concern to parents of children with asthma. A student at an inner-city school in a large Midwestern city described how she saw roaches in the lower level of the school where the cafeteria is located. Inner-city school administrators need to be aware of these issues and build regular extermination into their budgets.

Some children are born with respiratory ailments. Other children develop them as they grow. Regardless of when asthma develops, the condition must be managed. This is a major concern for parents of asthmatic children as they become school age, as parents have to ensure that their children have inhalers and other medications they need in school. Parents also have to ensure that their children understand their condition so that they know when they need to seek help.

School-aged children in the United States miss nearly fifteen million school days yearly due to asthma alone (Tarbis, Rammel, Huffman, and Taylor 2006). Most inner-city schools have predominately low-income minority student populations. African American children are three times more likely to die from asthma than other children (Levy, Heffner, Stewart, and Beeman 2006). Asthma also has a strong presence in low-income school environments that do not have a large number of minorities.

School nurses at inner-city schools are acutely aware of the need to manage asthma among student populations. It is paramount that they know who the asthmatic children are. Submitting medical forms to the school as soon as possible is vital. As soon as children are newly diagnosed with asthma, the parents should immediately notify their school. The situation becomes more complicated in those instances where the parent cannot be reached because the school does not have correct contact information.

Often parents do not have the complete knowledge of the extent of the condition and how to help manage it, so it is very important that school nurses can communicate easily with parents. Most parents, even those of poor inner-city children, have taken their asthmatic children for some professional care outside of the school environment. However, many inner-city children from low socioeconomic backgrounds seek medical attention at community clinics where they do not have a consistent attending physician with a relationship with and knowledge of the child's condition. Other parents tend to utilize the emergency room of the nearest hospital as their "doctor," and take their asthmatic child there when the child's condition escalates.

Many schools do not have a nurse available every day. One urban district in a large Midwestern city cannot afford to fund enough nurses for each school to have a full-time nurse. Therefore, each nurse may be responsible for covering at least two schools.

The lack of available nurses in a school should be of grave concern to parents of asthmatic children. It is very important for schools to have a plan to address the needs of asthmatic children, should an emergency or immediate need arise.

Schools usually have an inhaler available for acute attacks. One school administrator at an inner-city school in the Midwest advised that they have an inhaler and have become accustomed to using it with many children before physical education class because many of the students suffering from asthma were winded after class. This school also has a breathing machine for children who become severely winded.

For emergencies, schools do not hesitate to call 911. One boy who was severely asthmatic had no medication; his mother did not send the medication with him to school. The inhaler at the school did not relieve his symptoms, so after calling the mother and leaving a voicemail message, the school called 911. The boy was taken by ambulance to the hospital and was subsequently admitted. This happened in the morning, and it was late afternoon before the mother actually contacted the school. "She seemed very upset with us for calling 911 and that her son was admitted to the hospital," the principal said. "We told her we tried the inhalant and he had no medication, so we did the best we could, but she still seemed very upset with us. I'm not sure why."

Other conditions exist that affect an inner-city student's ability to excel in school. Or at the very least, these conditions should cause parents to be cautious and concerned.

Many children in inner-city schools have been diagnosed with attention-deficit/hyperactivity disorder (ADHD). Students with this condition have a difficult time concentrating and focusing on school. The condition appears to be more prevalent in boys than girls.

The diagnosis and treatment of ADHD has always been controversial. The highest rates of ADHD among school-aged children proportionally are reportedly in low-income and minority environments, with African American boys composing the majority of cases. There is some question as to what really constitutes a behavioral condition as opposed to what should be considered an action needing behavior modification. Some people argue, "All that boy needs is some disciplining," "The teacher needs to pay more attention to her," or "The teacher needs to encourage them." These same people might say that making a diagnosis and prescribing medication is the easy way out for parents, health professionals, and educators who do not want to do the hard work to help children overcome behavioral issues. ADHD will continue to be a topic of debate for the broader community.

But children are diagnosed with ADHD and prescribed medication. School nurses and staff administer the drugs to children in school on a regular basis.

The symptoms associated with ADHD are, more than many chronic diseases, directly linked to successful learning. Actually, ADHD is closely associated with learning disabilities. A recent national survey of special education students showed that children with ADHD are a rapidly growing group of students within special education programs (Schnoes, Reid, Wagner, and Marder 2006). Many parents of children with ADHD are dealing with a "double whammy." Not only do their children have a diagnosed health condition, but for most of them it has a direct impact on whether or not they are successful in school.

The condition of childhood obesity is a problem among children in schools across the country. The Centers for Disease Control and Prevention (CDC) reports that childhood obesity has increased threefold in the last thirty years. Inner-city schools are no exception. Generations of unhealthy eating, lack of healthy food in the vicinity of the inner city, unhealthy snacks within the school, and lack of adequate physical activity in and out of school are among contributing factors to obesity among children. Obesity can ultimately lead to all kinds of medical issues as a child progresses into adulthood, such as heart problems, diabetes, and cancer.

One nutritionist in a large Midwestern city talked about the influx of obesity in children she had observed in urban schools she worked in. "Many of them were overweight because of the kind of food they ate on a daily basis, not just in school, but often given to them at home," she said. She cited a study by a local health agency where they questioned hundreds of school-aged children, the majority of whom said they would be willing to try more healthy foods, but they were not getting them at home. Recently the CDC published a study on the link between healthy eating, physical activity, and improved academic performance. In the study, it was noted that schools that provided healthier foods, particularly those educational facilities that participated in the United States Department of Agriculture (USDA) School Breakfast Program (SBP), coupled with more physically activity, saw great increase in the academic grades and standardized test schools of their students. (CDC 2014).

A balanced diet helps children learn. Poor diets result in vitamin deficiencies, particularly B vitamins, and anemia, which can cause long-lasting neurological deficits when untreated (Armstrong 2010). Vitamin deficiencies are preventable if children have access to a variety of healthy foods such as lean meats, fresh fruits and vegetables, and low-fat dairy products.

The well-publicized achievement gap between children of various racial and socioeconomic groups may very well be diminished with a greater attention to diet in the disadvantaged groups. Some behavioral disorders that affect learning, like ADHD, can be more effectively managed with greater attention to a balanced diet or recognition of foods that might trigger a neurological reaction that inhibits learning.

Poverty is linked to poor health in children in many inner-city environments. In families with little access to fresh fruits and vegetables and healthy food options, their school-aged children may perform poorly in school because of lack of a balanced diet. However, when inner-city parents, even in poverty, have the capacity to make healthy food choices for their children, they should be doing so for the benefit of their children's learning abilities.

The nutritionist was also very concerned about the results of blood pressure screenings among the inner-city children. "Although a variety of children showed elevated blood pressure, many of the overweight children had higher than normal blood pressure," she said. "I immediately notified the parents, and suggested that they follow up with a physician."

Every year there seems to be a new strain of the flu that affects everyone, including children. Each year in the United States, on average thirty-six thousand people die from flu-related complications and more than two hundred thousand people are hospitalized from flu-related causes. The flu causes a significant amount of absenteeism in schools every year. The absenteeism is a concern for the academic well-being of the child, and may affect the ability of working mothers to get or maintain work if they need to find childcare.

The CDC and most health-related entities recommend that parents and their children receive vaccinations against the flu every year. Most schools now are being very deliberate about taking precautions to prevent the spread of flu in the schools, by advising children to cover their noses and mouths when sneezing and promoting frequent hand washing. Schools also work very hard to clean and disinfect areas where germs are prone to be present.

The H1N1 scare of 2009 was particularly disruptive. Its influence was widespread. Because H1N1, also known as *swine flu*, had reached pandemic level, school districts and health departments in many large cities dispatched emergency teams to schools to administer vaccines to the children. There was a great concern in the inner city for asthmatic children because people with other illnesses seemed more susceptible to the H1N1 virus. In one study, 57 percent of children who had been hospitalized as a result of 2009 H1N1 had also had one or more "higher risk" medical conditions. This point was from the following website: www.cdc.gov/h1n1flu/qa.htm. Asthma, along with pregnancy, diabetes, heart disease, and kidney disease were among the high-risk medical conditions that made people more susceptible to H1N1. With new strains of flu developing every year, educators continue to be aware of how epidemics can affect schools and school-aged children.

The bedbug epidemic does not discriminate due to socioeconomic status. However, this situation appears to be quite prevalent in many low-income, inner-city communities. Although bedbugs do not appear to carry or spread disease, the itchy bumps they leave can make children uncomfortable and may interfere with their ability to sleep. Children who do not get enough sleep may have problems getting up for school in the morning or concentrating while in school.

Parents of inner-city children with bedbugs may live in an environment where the landlord may have an exterminator eradicate the problem, or they may be expected to deal with the issue themselves. Parents may not have the funds to hire an exterminator. There is only so much washing in hot water and drying at 120 degrees that a family can do, especially in the case of an epidemic. And parents not only worry about the bedbug infestation that their family is enduring, but the infestations their children may bring home from other children in school.

The school usually cannot pinpoint who brought in the bedbugs. Often, it is difficult or impossible to determine which parents to notify, assuming a student brought the bedbugs into the school.

Lead poisoning in children has been associated with reduced intelligence, shortened memory, slower reaction types, poor hand-eye coordination, and antisocial behavior (Rothman, Lourie, and Gaughan 2002). This condition is of great concern to parents living in structures built before 1950. Those homes were often constructed using lead-based paint. Children living in those homes ingest dust and soil from the lead-based paint. Small children tend to put paint chips in their mouths. The lead poisoning tends to affect children under six more frequently.

An administrator in an urban school in a large Midwestern city said that lead poisoning is "a huge issue" at her school. She spoke of the large number of special needs children who have lead poisoning and its effects on their intellectual abilities. She spoke of the middle school children who have severe reading and emotional problems that have been attributed to lead poisoning.

Much of the problem with lead poisoning is that parents are not educated about lead and its effects. A three-year grassroots effort in an inner-city neighborhood in Philadelphia involving 1,200 children and 900 adults resulted in creative outreach and awareness programs. This effort resulted in significant reductions of lead levels in children and greatly heightened awareness among adults.

In chapter 5 there was discussion on scoliosis and the possible side affects of a delayed diagnosis. Scoliosis causes quality-of-life issues for children as they mature into adulthood and is better treated before children reach fifteen years old.

Dental issues can have a real impact on children. A painful toothache can hinder a child from being able to concentrate in school. It may make a child irritable and cause behavioral problems. Some school districts in inner cities see the need to take preventive actions. In one large Midwestern city, the health department sent out notices to the parents of second, fourth, and seventh graders to get written authorization for dental technicians to come to the school to apply a dental sealant to their children's teeth. The sealant prevents tooth decay and cavities. Sealants can last up to four years or more.

The need for braces is often a great concern for parents and their children. Sometimes the need for braces is more aesthetic than medical. Everyone wants to feel confident about their looks. Sometimes the need for braces is actual a medical concern. Often braces are associated with other facial and jaw conditions.

Dental braces are not cheap. The cost ranges from 3,000 to 5,000 dollars. Parents from low-income families may be able to get braces covered through government funding. However, those in the urban core who could be classified as "the working poor" may have more difficulty funding braces. If those individuals have health insurance through work, they normally find some difficulty as most major health insurance carriers pay a small "lifetime benefit" for braces. So parents often need to wrap their minds around the fact that they will have to contribute significant dollars of their own to afford braces for their children.

Many orthodontists will allow parents to make monthly payments. While it gets the braces in the child's mouth, it creates a substantial financial burden that takes years to satisfy.

Diabetes plagues many inner-city children. One inner-city school administrator in a large Midwestern city expressed great concern about the number of diabetic children in her school. Her concern was that when there were no nurses in the school, someone, usually a teacher, administrator, or office support staff member, had to administer shots to ailing children. "The parents send the meter in with the child to test their blood and if their sugar level is too low, we had to give them a shot," she said. "We had no choice—it's very disturbing, but we are responsible, not trained."

Mental health and learning disabilities in schools are much more frequently diagnosed and more evident than ever before. Children in the United States are suffering from an array of mental health disorders such as depression, anxiety, and ADHD. These appear to be the most psychiatric syndromes impacting children (Department of Health and Human Services 2000)

Urban children, particularly those individuals of lower socioeconomic status and those of color, experience hardships and circumstances that can contribute to poor mental health conditions. Yet it is the disadvantaged who, for various reasons, are less likely to get adequate or even any mental health services. In some schools, mental health services are not available. Some schools have limited services, perhaps only a day or two per week if a school psychologist is available. One urban school principal in a large Midwestern city said that they have a psychologist who only conducts testing for mental health conditions—she does no counseling.

Psychologists may not have the experience dealing with children of urban environments in low socioeconomic standing. Or they do not possess the cultural competence to deal with children of color who are so prevalent in inner-city environments. Some parents of inner-city children do not subscribe to the psychologist as a professional for their children.

Ms. Baker, the administrator of an inner-city school in a large Midwestern city where the majority of students are African American, has many students living in traumatic circumstances. They live in the midst of poverty, crime, drugs, and squalor, and for most of them, the best part of their day is coming to school.

An African American female, Ms. Baker believes that many of the students need psychological counseling, but their parents will not seek it for them. "African American parents historically don't take the counseling thing seriously," she said. "We used the Bible as our base of teaching what to do and what not to do in terms of lifelong learning." Ms. Baker is concerned that many of the families do not go to church or read the Bible regularly. So they have no standards to live by. Yet they will tell her they don't believe in counseling. "When they refuse my recommendation of counseling, I don't know what to offer them," she said. "I have suggested to a few parents that they need to go to church if they will not accept counseling for their child."

African Americans and other minorities in the inner city are likely to be the most underserved by mental health services. Because of their environmental and sociological surroundings, they may likely be the most in need of mental health services in terms of demographics, but the least served. The issue is not just that certain cultures may not be as open to mental health services, but also that mental health professionals who encounter minorities, particularly school-aged children, need to have the necessary cultural competencies to be effective in treating people of color.

Many children in inner-city schools are being treated for ADHD. Young African American boys in inner-city schools are being diagnosed with ADHD and given medications in what some would consider alarming proportions. The diagnosis and treatment of ADHD is very controversial. Young boys are given mind-altering drugs as if they have no potential long-term effects. Parents should be concerned.

Children living in homelessness appear to have a large amount of health challenges. Studies of children in sheltered, homeless families have shown that many have poor health status; high rates of asthma; high rates of emergency department visits; delays in obtaining preventive care; and high rates of emotional, developmental, and behavioral problems (Karr and Kline 2004).

It is likely that limited access to well-child care may be part of the reason why homeless children have more health issues. Certainly an inability to obtain preventive services would make a child susceptible to illness and medical conditions. Lack of a consistently balanced diet can compromise the immune system of a young child, opening that child up to many illnesses and conditions. And certainly the concerns associated with not having a stable home to go home to at night must be psychologically challenging for a child.

The lack of attention to immunizations by parents is prevalent in inner-city schools. According to one inner-city school principal in a large Midwestern city, parents are usually very good at getting the initial shots for their children. It is the follow-up, subsequent shots that often get missed. The principal said that they have a nurse check records once per year and for those children missing immunizations, their parents get a "ten-day letter," giving them ten days to bring back proof of immunizations or giving them an appointment date to get the shots. Those not doing either are told their children cannot come back to school until they have received their shots or can give an appointment date. In this particular school of six hundred students, at one point seventy-five children were out of compliance, and thus out of school.

Why would so many children be out of school for noncompliance with immunizations? One inner-city school principal offered several explanations. "Some parents do not take responsibility and I can't explain why," she said. "Some have jobs with no [insurance] benefits. Some are too concerned about getting fired from work for having to take off." This principal explained that sometimes the parents will send a note with the child opposing immunizations for religious beliefs or concerns about safety. In those cases, they will excuse the students from having the shots.

Many inner-city schools across the country have now partnered with health organizations to have medical clinics in the schools. One inner-city school principal described how she brought that about. "We partnered with the local children's hospital that was within a mile of the school," she said. "I wrote a grant to get the initial funding and we had the clinic built right into the school."

The principal described it as a "community clinic," open to the general public. By having a health clinic, the school contributed to the well-being of the neighborhood by providing a needed service to residents of the surrounding community. For example, on any given day, elderly men and women or working adults could be seen coming from the clinic. It was centrally located for residents and people working in the area.

Clinics within a school contribute greatly to their effectiveness. One principal described how having a clinic in the school helped reduce attendance problems because children could be treated onsite if necessary, and sent back to class if they were all right. "One boy had what appeared to us to be a severe asthma attack and we took him downstairs to the clinic," he recalled. "They were able to treat him and send him back to class."

One study showed that students not enrolled in a school-based health clinic (SBHC) lost three times as much seat time in school as students enrolled in an SBHC (Van Cura 2010). In an era where many schools are funded based on the number of children in attendance, an SBHC seems like a great idea.

Clinics are also able to take preventive measures, like providing flu shots and vaccinations, with written consent from parents. Preventive healthcare also significantly affects attendance. While flu shots and other vaccinations are strictly a personal choice made by parents for their children, their effectiveness in keeping more children well and in school is well documented.

Often children have prescribed medications that they do not have in school for some reason. Maybe a child has a headache and needs a pain reliever. Or maybe a child has an acute or chronic condition that needs attention. They can easily and safely be treated in a clinic located in the school by qualified personnel.

However, there are many urban schools without clinics. Moreover, there are many schools that do not have nurses on duty every day. Many schools do not have nurses at all. Often when funding is tight, budgets for school nurses do not make the cut. In lean economic times, schools often make decisions that involve saving as many positions as possible that are more directly related to instruction.

The fact that many urban schools lack adequate medical professionals should be of serious concern to parents. One administrator who spent years in urban public schools and is now in an urban charter school said not having nurses was an ongoing phenomenon that she had experienced in the inner-city schools for many years. "If a child came into the office sick and we didn't know how to help him, we might just tell him to lay down, or if he had a cut we'd give him a bandage, and depending on the severity of their condition, we might call 911," she said. "If we couldn't reach the parents, we'd let the paramedics make the decision on how to treat the child."

Another inner-city school principal talked about how main office staff, including herself and the clerical employees, administer medicine, give asthmatic children an inhaler or breathing treatments, and even give diabetic children shots even though they have no formal training. "That's just the way it is," she said. "We do to help the kids." She admitted that most parents probably do not understand that they are entrusting their children to medically untrained staff. They drop off their children, sometimes with medication and sometimes not, along with a note telling when to give the medication to the child. "Most parents never even asked us any questions—they just dropped off their kids," she said.

But parents should be asking questions. Why are untrained office staff giving medical assistance? Why are school teachers, administrators, and clerical workers administering shots? Why are they being entrusted with making what could be life-or-death decisions regarding children? It seems irresponsible that school systems would allow this to continue. The question parents should be asking school systems is why is an emphasis on health not considered part of the instruction and institutional effectiveness of the school?

Central administration of the schools should look at the academic progress of the school versus the overall health of children. In most urban school districts, the worst-performing schools have the least access to professional health services. That is why so many schools throughout the country are incorporating health clinics into the buildings.

Not all health concerns of children require a great deal of attention; however, most school districts limit what kinds of services can be offered without some kind of formal approval process. For example, a seventh grade girl with severe menstrual pain could not concentrate in her classes at an urban school in a large Midwestern city. Finally, after spending half the day in agony and really not paying much attention to her teachers, she went to the nurse's office. The nurse was authorized to give her some Midol tablets to relieve her symptoms.

All schools should have meticulous records documenting issues related to the health of each child. They should have records of nurses having seen each child for whatever reason. They should have records on immunizations. This information is especially important for inner-city schools because of the number of ailing children. Teachers or other personnel depend on accurate and up-to-date health records to be able to handle issues for children as they emerge. And the fact that most do not have a nurse at the school every day dictates that other school personnel may need to access children's records at any time.

In addition, because of the mobility of students in the urban school environment, records that are kept at one school could be helpful to a receiving school. Having that kind of history could conceivably save the life of a child, or at the very least be able to assist the receiving school in meeting the academic, physiological, and psychological needs of a child new to the school.

Lack of adequate professional health services in schools is a substantial barrier to academic achievement. Students spend less time in classroom instruction if there is no adequate system for dealing with their health issues—they may be sent home or to a medical facility, or they may, for example, have to schedule time during the school day to visit a doctor offsite to treat a chronic or acute condition. A child who is sick or in pain may not be as astute in the classroom as he or she would be if well.

Having a qualified medical professional in the building also minimizes the risk that nonqualified personnel will make a mistake to the detriment of the child. What if an office secretary incorrectly gives a diabetic child a shot that causes a serious reaction? What if a staff member gives a student the wrong dosage of a life-saving medication? What if a student suffers a fall and no one knows how to treat him? Schools reduce the liability associated with treating children by having qualified medical personnel available as much as possible.

A qualified health professional also allows other personnel to perform in their areas of expertise. For example, a principal who is constantly focused on specific health concerns of children cannot effectively operate as the chief executive of the entire school. A teacher who is administering first aid to a student cannot teach her class. Support staff who are giving shots or administering medication to a child cannot answer the phone.

REFLECTIONS

Health considerations are among the most significant factors in the successful education of children. Serious medical conditions can hinder learning in children. For various reasons, inner-city children are more susceptible to many health-related conditions. Often they do not have the access to onsite medical services, such as school nurses, that a middle-class school environment may have. Educators are well served to have some knowledge of common conditions they may encounter in school children so that they can recognize them and determine the level of support needed to resolve their situations. Educators and parents must work together to ensure that student health needs are met so that they can achieve academic success.

EIGHT

Making Parent Involvement
Successful in Inner-City Schools

Throughout this book, we have stressed that the inner-city school environment is truly unique. Without question, many urban schools are failing. Children in urban schools are lagging behind children academically in the United States and in countries around the world, although the United States guarantees a free education through grade twelve for every child.

Experts have been preaching about the importance of parent involvement in schools for years. Researchers have done many studies showing the benefits of parent involvement at various levels on the academic and emotional well being of children. For example, a recent study demonstrated that parental involvement, emotional well-being of students, and their academic achievement are all interrelated on one level or another (Henderson and Mapp, 2001). Similar findings were revealed in a 2003 study by scholars Nestor M. Arguea and Stephen J. Conroy, who analysis showed how the development of effective parental involvement had a differ relationship to the emotional mindset and academic achievement on fifth graders at a local elementary school in several urban schools in Florida (Arguea and Conroy, 2003). However, educators who are focused on supporting and improving the direct educational activities performed by the teachers may miss the total picture, the total environment that creates the optimum learning situation for the child.

Parent involvement is not the only solution to the failure to schools in America. The thought of overhauling the entire educational system is daunting. The problems are different, depending on whose perspective one is looking at. Some say it's the teachers. They are not educated enough or they are not dedicated enough or the best potential teachers are going into business and industry since they do not get enough pay as teachers. Or teachers are not performing at an optimum level because they are not on a pay-for-performance system.

Some say poor-performing schools are the fault of the teacher unions that fight for so many concessions for teachers that they undermine the educational process. Some say that teachers in some communities make so much money and benefits that the system cannot afford supplies or extra teachers or specialists to help children learn better. Some say that because of the systems put in place, terminating the inadequate teachers is very difficult.

Some blame the lack of the newest educational techniques that enhance the teachers' or schools' abilities to take the teaching to the next level. The lack of time for adequate professional development is also related to this situation. The list is endless but the most important issues are the lack of money, inadequate administrators, poor facilities, and crowded classrooms.

There is no one easy solution to the dilemma of how to effectively educate children. Addressing any one of these issues is like putting a bandage on the wound, but failing to address the cause of the wound at its core. It is like treating the symptoms and not the illness as a whole.

The question is whether the educational system is willing to look at the big picture. Does the system have the conviction to trust parents to be part of the educational process? Does the system have the courage to go beyond what is considered appropriate and try different solutions?

Here are some solutions that are specifically tailored to the urban inner-city school setting. Some will require people to think and act in ways contrary to the way they were taught. While in concept these ideas could work anywhere, they are especially conceptualized for the inner-city school environment.

1. HELP PARENTS HELP THEMSELVES

Often parents lack the knowledge or skills to better themselves, their children, and their surroundings. Within most schools are the knowledge, resources, and influences to help parents achieve heights that they may feel they cannot achieve on their own.

Parents who feel empowered can display a new confidence in their ability to be successful. They can be strong role models for their children.

- A large number of parents of children in inner-city schools have never finished school themselves. Schools should consider organizing GED training sessions at the schools. Imagine the confidence of a mother who finally earns a GED and can confidentially interact with her children as a high school graduate.
- Hold some parent training sessions that can assist parents with developing professional skills.

- Ms. Thompson was a parent coordinator at an inner-city school in a large Midwestern city. She frequently held Internet and email training sessions at the school's parent center. She also sponsored several resume writing sessions and was able to get help from a local organization to provide parents with donated professional clothes for job interviewing.
- Host a college information session for parents at the school. Local community colleges and four-year institutions with programs geared toward nontraditional adult learners are often looking for creative ways to reach out to prospective students.
- Host various trainings on ways parents can assist their children. One school brought in an expert on the individualized education plan (IEP) process to teach parents with children with special needs how to advocate for their children. One mother talked about her experience at an IEP meeting after having attended such a session. She said that because she knew more about what was supposed to happen, and spoke out in the IEP meeting, two of the three teachers in attendance got frustrated and left the meeting. But ultimately as a result, she was able to demand and receive more specialized services for her son.
- Many school systems mandate that each school has a site council that operates similar to some boards of directors or trustees. Usually these school site councils are required to have one or more parents as members. In one large Midwestern city, an elementary school site council's parent representative was also a teacher, which made the site council look suspect to parents. Make sure at least one parent representative to the site council is not an employee at the school.
- One parent coordinator at an inner-city school in a Midwestern city was concerned about the lack of crossing guards in the vicinity of the school. She found out that the city was responsible for hiring the crossing guards and that they were looking to hire a few around her school. She communicated that to some parents who she knew were looking for extra money, and three of them were hired as crossing guards.

2. HOST PARENT ACTIVITIES IN UNLIKELY PLACES

Many activities to which parents are invited take place at the schools, which is okay because schools have the facilities to handle groups. However, often parents of inner-city school children are not comfortable in schools for various reasons, mostly related to their discomfort because of their own lack of success in school or their discomfort interacting with educators.

Schools should partner with community centers or other organizations to host activities. These organizations could host enrichment or fitness activities for parents, or even free health screenings. YMCAs, YWCAs, and recreation centers often welcome community partnerships that will help them reach more people or give greater access to their resources. Some organizations may agree to give special discounts or incentives to parents from the school who sign up for their programs.

Churches can provide attractive partnerships for schools. Churches have facilities that are often accommodating to sizeable groups and that may be available on opportune days and times.

Many churches have members who are professionals who can provide free or reduced services to families. Some churches have counseling services that can help parents and families in crisis. One large inner-city church in a Midwestern city sponsors a series of free financial planning services and first-time homebuyers' seminars for the surrounding community. Another inner-city church in the same city has a health and wellness ministry that offers free blood pressure screenings monthly and holds health fairs and presentations that are open to the entire community.

Nightclubs and bars are plentiful in the inner city and for many provide a positive source for entertainment. Those venues have access to parents of inner-city school children. Why not host events at a local club to demonstrate an outreach to parents? Having the courage to go beyond what is considered appropriate is going to be how schools change. Bars and nightclubs can easily accommodate social gatherings that could build trust among parents and educators. Sometimes these establishments even allow organizations to raise money by donating a portion of food and drink sales or cover charges to the organization. This could be a great fundraiser for a parent or school group.

Restaurants could be a nice place to gather parents. Of course, depending on the restaurant, a sizeable cost could be incurred when buying meals for parents and their children that they may bring along, but the benefits could be great. One lead teacher in an inner-city school recalled how she wanted to talk with a particular parent about her daughter's performance in her class. She picked up the mother and five children and treated them all to McDonald's for dinner, and had a productive meeting with the mother. The child eventually became one of the highest performers in her math class.

3. PARTNER WITH PROFESSIONALS

Professionals in the community with skills that can benefit parents may enjoy volunteering a few hours if asked. It is just a matter of knowing the student and parent population and finding the professionals who will be willing to take a little time to help,

Children get colds, flu, and other illnesses. Many children suffer from asthma, diabetes, and other serious conditions. Environmental conditions trigger allergies and other ailments. A doctor, nurse, or public health professional could really be an interesting and beneficial speaker for parents. The person may not be able to give specific medical advice, but he or she usually has valuable information of use to parents and their children.

Someone who can answer legal questions always appeals to parents, regardless of whether they live in the inner city or not. The Legal Aid Society in many cities will often send lawyers out to speak to groups. Sometimes they will focus on one particular issue, or they will present and field questions on a variety of issues. One inner-city school in a Midwestern city had a Legal Aid attorney come to the school to speak to parents and answer questions about landlord-tenant issues.

Sometimes parents can benefit from talking to someone who can provide resources and counseling. Social workers are excellent at conducting presentations on issues of concern to parents and children. Many schools have at least a part-time social worker in the building. Many public and private organizations have access to social workers who can interact with parents and direct them to needed resources.

Many parents can use free financial advice. Bankers and other financial consultants often speak to groups as a service to the community. Some banks will even make special offers to groups as a result. Especially popular are custodial savings accounts for children that usually require a very small minimum deposit and that must bear the name of both child and parent.

Economic conditions have rendered many parents unemployed or underemployed. Public and private organizations that can provide job coaching, career advising, or employment assistance to parents would be a valuable resource for schools to offer. For example, the Urban League in most cities does outreach into communities and may agree to host a workshop or seminar for parents at a local school.

Many parents are interested in higher education opportunities. Most colleges and universities have recruiters who go out into the community and make presentations about their programs. Success in higher education can truly be an empowering experience for parents, who with a degree can vie for employment or better career opportunities.

4. EDUCATORS AT THE HIGHEST LEVELS HAVE TO LOOK AT THE WHOLE PROBLEM

Educators have to have the courage to focus globally on the welfare of children first. They need to believe that parents are part of the solution. They have to accept that the welfare of the parent and the family are as important as the welfare of the student. The evidence is all there, although some educators seem not to see it or seem not to want to see it. Look at the parents in the high-performing suburban schools. Most have at least a high school education, with most having some college, with good incomes, houses, and cars. And while there are always exceptions, educated middle- to upper-class environments are synonymous with high academically performing schools.

So much money, professional development, and emphasis goes into improving teaching techniques and instructional resources. Those expenses are usually justified. However, not enough resources go into addressing family situations and providing opportunities for improvement, which directly affects how much students can excel. When parents are incorporated into the educational process, children progress on many levels.

The home is the foundation for a child. Some children will excel regardless of their surroundings. However, focus on activities that help build strong families can only enhance the educational process. Funding for family activities and parent outreach should be as prominent a priority in the budget and objectives as instructional programs and initiatives.

5. ACCEPT THAT THIS IS A LONG, SLOW PROCESS

Developing parental involvement may take years of work and suffer lots of setbacks. The thought of not educating children who want to be educated is unconscionable. Some parents do not want to be involved and will not participate, regardless of the circumstances. That happens in the best of schools. The goal is to get as many parents as possible who want to be involved, and hope that these actions will attract several that were not active before or would not have been active otherwise. Establish a reasonable goal for parental involvement and work to achieve that. If that goal is exceeded, it is all the better.

The process of engaging parents is never ending. The reality is, most involved parents follow their children. So for example, when an eighth grader graduates to the ninth grade and to high school, active parents in the middle school will likely cease to be active in the middle school. So educators have to make recruiting and outreach of parents a continuous activity.

In the case of inner-city schools, where there can be so much mobility, educators have to get used to having involved parents at one point and having a new set of involved parents at another point, or having to continually recruit new parents because families move so much. In addition, as families goes through economic crises, parents may be active intermittently, but take time off to handle their personal issues.

Dealing with parent involvement and outreach in the inner city cannot be about numbers. So many organizations and agencies and funding sources are focused on the concept of "return on investment." Many times parent activities are abandoned or considered a failure because a few parents showed up, as opposed to a few dozen, or a few hundred. Those few parents that do continually show up deserve the best possible attention and support. If they have a good experience, they may go back and tell many more parents. There is something to be said for the grapevine effect.

Sometimes expectations are based on how suburban school parent attendance might look, which is not a fair comparison. Most suburban schools have resources that the inner-city schools do not have. They have money to engage parents. They have active parents who can afford to give time to the school, and participate in the education of their children. The kinds of crises and experiences that an urban parent has that causes barriers to effective parent involvement and engagement may not exist in the suburban school environment.

6. ESTABLISH A PARENT ORGANIZATION WITHOUT TEACHERS

Many parents are not comfortable with teachers. Including teachers may discourage many parents from being a part of a parent group. It would be more effective to give the parents some general guidelines for what they may want to accomplish, and let them evolve into their own support group. It is better to have a group of consistent, committed parents than to lose or fail to attract parents because of an agenda set by teachers or administrators that the parents do not understand or appreciate.

Often parent–teacher groups in inner-city schools end up having as many or more teachers than parents. These organizations were designed to be parent-driven, but when teachers end up dominating the numbers and the agenda, parents are less likely to take part.

This is not a knock against Parent–Teacher Associations and Organizations (PTAs/PTOs). These organizations have done much good in schools all over the country. However, when teachers control the PTO, parents feel marginalized and helpless. An organization for parents should make them feel empowered to be involved in the education of their children and support of the school. A parent organization in an inner-city school would be better served by having a parent coordinator to oversee their activities than by having teachers involved who may dominate the agenda with their own interests.

An inner-city school in a Midwestern city had a consistent group of about fifteen parents who showed up once per week at about 1 p.m. All were women; most were single mothers. The parent coordinator was the only school representative who was actually part of the group. This group of committed parents decided to have their own book club, and every week they discussed a particular book they had selected to read.

The parent coordinator indicated that the parents seemed to have more of an interest in the welfare of the school because they were in the building regularly, and their discussions often turned to issues of concern of the school in addition to the books. She was able to communicate to the principal concerns around safety and security in the building, maintenance issues like nonfunctioning sinks and toilets, and issues with specific teachers.

As a result of the parent coordinator's discussions with the principal regarding feedback from the parents, substantial changes were made in the school. The principal was able to work through the district office and the local police department to get a police officer in the building who was able to maintain order in the school, while still befriending students and giving them drug and safety seminars.

7. LEARN THE COMMUNITY SURROUNDING THE SCHOOL

Embrace the neighborhood of which the school is a part. Make sure the teachers know the community in great detail. Make the history and development of the community part of a teacher in-service day or professional development day. Every employee in the school—including maintenance, lunchroom workers, office workers, crossing guards, and everyone who has some part in the workings of the school—should know the community's demographics, geography, politics, socioeconomic, environmental issues, real estate, social justice issues, and so on.

The better school employees understand the neighborhood surrounding a school, the more they can understand and embrace students and their families. Dr. Jones, the principal at Roosevelt School, recalled that when he first got to the school, drug dealers frequented the playground and parking lot at all hours of the day (even during school hours) and night. The grounds were sometimes littered by morning with beer cans, liquor bottles, and drug paraphernalia.

Dr. Jones appealed to the drug dealers by introducing himself to them, describing to them his vision for a better school for the children, and asking them to stay clear of the grounds but to keep watch over the children. The drug dealers agreed to stay across the street from the school. They accepted their role as protectors of the children, and Dr.

Jones recalled situations where a drug dealer would come into the school to warn him if they thought they saw someone questionable on the grounds.

8. REQUIRE OR STRONGLY RECOMMEND PARENT INVOLVEMENT

A parent involvement requirement, even if not enforceable, establishes a goal for parents. Many parents are not sure how to get involved or how they will fit the involvement into their schedule. Giving parents something to plan for may increase the amount of involvement in the school. Maybe it is a recommended number of hours, such as three hours per year. Maybe it is a recommended number of events per years, such as two conferences or two parent meetings. The incentive for participating could include a culminating event at the end of the year where parents are recognized for their participation.

Schools that have contracts or requirements for parent or family involvement had great success increasing the numbers of participation in middle class or suburban schools. Even several parents that donate just a few hours per year can amount to hundreds of hours of involvement that would not have happened otherwise. And if the time commitment is reasonable, then parents are more apt to go for it.

9. PARENT SURVEYS AND FOCUS GROUPS

Often parents feel like educators do not really care what they think. They feel like they are being dictated to. They feel unappreciated. They feel devalued. Efforts to find out what is important to parents makes them feel they have some input in the process.

A survey to parents should be short, with no more than ten multiple choice questions and a section for comments. The administration of the survey should have multiple pathways. For example, there should be surveys at the office for parents to fill out who come into the building. Parent organization members should complete surveys. Perhaps the parent organization can arrange for some volunteers to help administer surveys to parents who come in the building or onto the grounds to pick up their young children. Surveys can be available for parent–teacher conferences and school events. Volunteers can call and get survey answers over the phone. The parents who have Internet access can get the surveys via email. All of these can go along with traditional methods such as U.S. mail and sending surveys home with students.

Reading feedback, especially if it is critical, is not easy. Often one finds out that certain actions or activities that seem good may be perceived totally differently by parents. Perceptions that someone cares by the act of collecting feedback is valuable for awhile. But some sort of follow-up is critical once results are sorted, reviewed, and evaluated. Some sort of presentation to parents is a necessity. Written results to parents are important and should be done. But some sort of formal event where results are presented to a group of parents, along with changes if there are any, should be done.

Organizing a focus group of parents can be a daunting task, but the rewards could be limitless. Perhaps it is a small group of five to seven parents. Or perhaps a larger group of twenty to thirty parents could be divided into smaller groups of five to seven with multiple group facilitators.

However the event is structured, small groups of parents interacting together regarding issues and concerns as well as ideas for improvements can be an invaluable source of information for a school principal. Parents will open up with other parents and strangers about all sorts of things that they may not feel comfortable saying around the principal or a teacher.

Sometimes an administrator will get more information just by working a crowd of parents. At the schools with large numbers of small children, an opportune time to for administrators to talk with parents is when the parents meet their children at the door of the school to walk them home; administrators can chat with parents to ask how their child is doing and what the school could do to make their experience better. Most parents just appreciate being asked. Potential criticism is not always easy to hear, but can be helpful to administrators.

Probably one of the most difficult realities about gathering large amounts of data that can be acquired in surveys and focus groups is the enormous amount of great ideas that come out of the process. These types of data-gathering experiences will generate more potential opportunities than a school can realistically handle in a year. It is important to develop a process for addressing the data and options so that contributors do not feel that their efforts were in vain.

Perhaps a group of parents could be led through a process of sifting through all the possibilities to determine what is doable and what is not. Ideally, before the parents get to the list, the administrator has already "triaged" the data and determined what initiatives can easily be acted upon. For example, one school was very close to a small corner store. Children would stop at the store on the way to school and buy snacks and bring them into the school. Feedback from parents was that they wish their children did not have that option of spending money on the way to school. The principal was able to convince the store owner to open the store thirty minutes later, after the start of school. In this case, the storeowner was willing and able to sacrifice some income for the good of the students and the school.

The effort of collecting surveys would be wasted if no actions were ever taken. Careful planning should be made to determine how to best act on the data.

10. SPONSOR A FAMILY EVENT WITH ENTERTAINMENT AND CHILDCARE

Often people ask what performances and parties at the school have to do with academic achievement. They say school-sponsored social events are not going to raise test scores. Maybe not, at least not directly. But much that is wrong in society now gets directly attributed to the breakdown of the family. Perhaps if education helps to promote family, society will be better served.

School-sponsored family events like performances by children, including plays, musical concerts, and talent shows, always attract families. Events like those do not just appeal to the parents, but often siblings and other relatives; even family friends will attend. One inner-city school had a play involving all the first graders. One boy in the play had ten family members present in the audience. An elderly lady in the audience was present because several children living on her street were in the play.

Another inner-city school had a spring concert where the various music classes sang. About forty-five parents showed up. The principal took about ten minutes prior to the start of the concert to talk about upcoming events, namely the upcoming state standardized testing the following week. He advised the parents to make sure their children got ample rest, and got to school on time.

Another way of getting everyone in the family involved is to have a Friday evening family event where the children are separated from the parents. Childcare should be provided for the youngest children. For middle school and older, organized games or movies can be provided. The parents should be separated into another area and be involved in some social activity, such as showing a movie parents would enjoy seeing or hosting an inspirational speaker. This should be a social event to lighten the spirits of the parents and make them feel comfortable being in the school building.

If it is possible to locate a "celebrity" to motivate parents and families, that would be a plus. One high school was able to get one of its graduates who had become a professional football player to come to an evening event at the school and give a motivational speech to parents and children. Over 150 parents and students attended the event.

For these events to have optimum attendance, they should include food, which should consist of a full meal and not just snacks. Food is a necessary expense. Food promotes fellowship and camaraderie.

Understanding the demographics of the families of a school and its surrounding community can help determine what kinds of activities may attract the most families. For example, if 50 percent of the families have children ranging in age from infants through five years old, then providing nursery care for events may attract more families. If many families have no car and they have to come at least two miles or more, perhaps transportation can be provided.

Or if there are significant numbers of families with active fathers or fathers in the home, why not sponsor the showing of a major sporting event at the school? Renting a large screen television and having pizza and hot dogs is a relatively small expense compared with the benefit of getting more fathers in the building.

Just understanding more about the demographics of the neighborhood would help to gage the potential interests of parents. For example, in a neighborhood filled with crime, drugs, and prostitution, parents may come out to hear a presentation from or have a meeting with the chief of police or a representative to get perceptions on crime in the area or to update parents on new measures that may be taking place. Every parent wants safety for themselves and their children. Such an event could attract a large gathering.

11. A PARENT COORDINATOR

Teachers and administrators just do not have the time to dedicate to parent involvement issues, so it's helpful to have a parent coordinator who focuses solely on parental issues. Parent involvement activities require significant planning, outreach, follow up, implementation, and maintenance. To be effective, parent involvement really cannot be done by someone who is doing it as an extra duty.

But the fact is, generating funding for a parent involvement professional may not be an option in tough economic times. School systems will consider what expenses they have to have, and often parent coordinator–type positions are near the top of the list to be eliminated. If hiring a parent coordinator is budget prohibitive, there may be some creative ways to acquire someone to do the work until funding conditions improve:

- Contact a local community organization with a similar mission and see if they have a person in a similar position who could incorporate the school parent involvement initiative into the organization's activities. The United Way in a large Midwestern city funded a "lead agency" initiative, where community-based organizations were funded to provide personnel to do outreach activities with parents and the community of select inner-city schools, under the oversight of each school's principal.

- Contact local colleges for special programs or internships that could provide staff or students to perform parent involvement outreach initiatives. Unfortunately, internships may not be very long, but could be a good tool for developing new initiatives. Students involved in internships will generally work well because they need an acceptable level of performance and a sign-off from the internship site to get a passing grade. They may not last long, however, usually between six and twenty weeks.
- Contact local churches or faith-based organizations for possibilities. Some churches have educational programs or volunteers that can assist with parent outreach. Many churches have initiatives that are geared toward family engagement.
- Find a community volunteer or volunteer parent who will organize or implement outreach activities. Some people who are retired volunteer because they can afford to do so. Some stay-at-home mothers or fathers may be interested in helping out in a school. Some volunteer organizations may be able to provide contact information for volunteers who sign up to work with them.

12. ESTABLISH A PARENT CENTER

Many schools now devoted a room to parents. A parent center could be a place that parents who normally are not comfortable in schools will come into and spend time. Dr. Jones, the principal of Roosevelt, created a parent center from an empty classroom. The parent center was equipped with couches and chairs, computers, a microwave oven, a refrigerator, and a sink. Every morning, fresh coffee and donuts were available for parents. Dr. Jones recalled that parents who never came into the building before were coming into the parent center.

One of the lead teachers at Roosevelt noticed that parental present in the school picked up significantly after the parent center opened. "Parents come into the center during the school day just to visit," she said. "They even come in to work on the computers." "As a result, many more parents visited the school more regularly for a variety of reasons. Without question, just with the addition of such a center, hundreds of parents viewed the facility as a much more caring and nurturing environment in which their students' would learn a great deal of valuable information as well as reach their potential."

References

Abernathy, Scott F. "Charter Schools, Parents, and Public Schools in Minnesota." *CURA Reporter* 34, no. 1 (2004): 1–7.

Abdule-Adil, Jaleel K. and Alvin David Farmer, Jr. 2006. Inner-City African American Parental Involvement in Elementary Schools: Getting Beyond Urban Legends of Apathy. *School Psychology Quarterly* 21, no. 1: 1–12.

Almy, Sarah, and Christina Theokas "Not Prepared for Class: High-Poverty Schools Continue to Have Fewer In-Field Teachers." *The Education Trust*, November 2010. Available from http://www.edtrust.org/dc/publication/not-prepared-for-class-high-poverty-schools-continue-to-have-fewer-in-field-teachers.

American Academy of Child and Adolescent Psychiatry. "Grandparents Raising Grandchildren." *Facts for Families*, no. 77 (March 2011). Available from http://www.aacap.org/AACAP/Families_and_Youth/Facts_for_Families/Facts_for_Families_Pages/Grandparents_Raising_Grandchildren_77.aspx.

Arguea, Nestor M. and Stephen J. Conroy. 2003. The Effect of Parental Involvement in Parent Teacher Groups on Student Achievement. *The School Community Journal* 13, no. 2: 119–136.

Armstrong, Alice. "Myths of Poverty: Realities for Students." *Education Digest* November/December 2009. Available from http://www.iaob.com/journal/j111209_02.cfm.

Bailyn, Bernard. 1960. *Education in the Forming of American Society: Needs and Opportunity of Study.* Chapel Hill: The University of North Carolina Press, 11

Barton, Angela C., Corey Drake, Jose Perez, Kathleen St. Louis, and Magnia George. 2004. Ecologies of Parental Engagement in Urban Education. *Educational Researcher* 33, no. 4: 3–12.

Baum, Angela C. and Paula McMurry-Schwartz 2004. Preserve Teachers Beliefs and Family Involvement: Implications for Teacher Education. *Early Childhood Education Journal* 32, no. 1: 57–61.

Beaulieu, John E. and Alex Granzin. 1999. *Working parents can raise smart kids.* Tacoma, WA: Parkland Press, Inc.

Benson, Forrest, and Sean Martin. "Organizing Successful Parent Involvement in Urban Schools." *Child Study Journal* 33, no. 3 (2003), 187–193.

Bloom, Leslie R. 2001. "I'm poor, I'm single, I'm a mom, and I deserve respect:" advocating in schools as and with mothers in poverty Educational Studies. 32, no. 3: 300–316.

Borman, Geoffrey, Samuel C. Stringfield, and Robert E. Slavin. 2001. *Title I. compensatory education at the crossroads.* Mahwah, NJ: Lawrence Erlbaum Associates, Inc.

Bowles, Samuel and Herbert Gintis (1976) *Schooling in Capitalist America* New York: Basic Books.

Burton, Drake, Perez, St. Louis, and George. 2004.

Bush, George W. "Remarks to the Fourth National Summit on Fatherhood." Washington, D.C.: National Fatherhood Initiative, June 7, 2001. Available from http://www.presidency.ucsb.edu/ws/index.php?pid=45956.

Carey, Nancy. 1998. *Parent involvement in children's education: Efforts by public elementary schools.* Department of Education.

Cohen. 1974. A History of Colonial Education, 1607 – 1776 New York: John Wiley and Sons, Inc.

Coleman, James S. 1966. *Equality of Educational Opportunity.* Washington, D.C.: GPO.

Constantino, Steven M. 2003. *Engaging All Families: Creating a Positive School Culture by Putting Research into Practice* Lanham, Maryland: Scarecrow Education.

Cubberly, Ellwood. 1934. *Public Education in the United States: A Study and Interpretation of American Educational History.* Boston: Houghton Mufflin.

Desimone, Laura. 1999. Linking parent involvement with student achievement: do race and income matter? *The Journal of Educational Research*, 93, no 1: 11–30.

Delpit, Lisa. 1994. Seeing color: A review of White teacher. In B. Bigelow, L. Christensen, S. Karp, B. Miner, and B. Parkerson (Eds.), *Rethinking our classrooms: Teaching for equity and justice* (pp. 130–131). Milwaukee, WI: Rethinking Schools.

Department of Health and Human Services. 2000.

Eberly, Christopher. 2002. Keeping the Promise of "No Child Left Behind;" Success or Failure Depends Largely on Implementation by the U.S. Department of Education. Harvard University: Harvard Civil Rights Project.

Elementary and Secondary Education Act (No Child Left Behind) of 2004.

Epstein, Joyce. 2001. *School, Family, and Community Partnerships: Preparing Educators and Improving Schools.* Boulder, CO: Westview Press.

Fine, Michelle. 1994. *Chartering Urban School Reform: Reflections on Public High Schools in the Midst of Change.* Williston, VT: Teachers College Press.

Feuerstein, Abe. 2000. School characteristics and parent involvement: Influences on participation in children's schools. *The Journal of Educational Research*, 94, no. 1: 29–39.

Fleischman, Howard L, Paul J. Hopstock, Marisa P. Pelczar, and Brooke E. Shelley, *Highlights From PISA 2009: Performance of U.S. 15-Year-Old Students in Reading, Mathematics, and Science Literacy in an International Context* (NCES 2011-004). U.S. Department of Education, National Center for Education Statistics. Washington, DC: U.S. Government Printing Office, 2010.

Forbis, Shalini, Jennifer Rammel, Belinda Huffman, and Robert Taylor. 2006. Barriers to Care of Inner-City Children with Asthma: School Nurse Perspective. *Journal of School Health* 76, no. 6: 205–207.

Ford, Richard Thompson. 2008. *The Race Card: How Bluffing about Bias Makes Race Relations Worse.* Farrar, Straus, and Giroux.

Gladstone, James W. and Ralph A. Brown. 2002. Grandparent involvement in child welfare intervention with grandchildren. *Elder's Advisor*, 4, no. 1: 11–18.

Gonzalez, Manny John. "Access to Mental Health Services: The Struggle of Poverty Affected Urban Children of Color." *Child and Adolescent Social Work Journal* 22, no. 3–4 (2005), 245–256.

Griffith, James. 1996. Relation of parental involvement, empowerment and school traits to student academic performance. *The Journal of Educational Research*, 90, no. 1, 33–41.

Gutman, Leslie and Carol Midgley. 2000. The role of protective factors in supporting the academic achievement of poor African American students during the middle school transition. *Journal of Youth and Adolescence*, 29, no. 2: 223–249.

Hacker, Andrew. 1992. *Two Nations: Separate, Hostile, and Unequal.* New York: Charles Scribner's Sons.

Hampton, Frederick, Dawne Mumford, and Lloyd Bond. 1998. Parent involvement in inner-city schools: the Project FAST extended family approach to success. *Urban Education*, 33, no. 3: 410–427.

Hayslip, Bert J. and Julie H. Patrick. 2006. *Custodial Grandparenting: Individual, Cultural, and Ethnic Diversity.* New York: Springer Publishing Company.

Henderson, Anne T. and Karen L. Mapp. 2001. *A new wave of evidence: The impact of school, family, and community connections on student achievements.* Austin, TX: Southwest Educational Development Laboratory.

Hill, Nancy E. and Stacie A. Craft. 2003. Parent-school involvement and school performance mediated pathways among socioeconomically comparable African American and Euro American families. *Journal of Educational Psychology*, 95, no. 1: 74–83.

Hill, Jason G., and Kerry J. Gruber. *Education and Certification Qualifications of Departmentalized Public School-Level Teachers of Core Subjects: Evidence from the 2007–08 Schools and Staffing Survey.* NCES 2011-317. Washington, D.C.: U.S. Department of Education, May 2011.

Izzo, Charles, Roger P. Weissberg, Wesley J. Kasprow, and Michael Fendrich. 1999. A longitudinal assessment of teacher perceptions of parental involvement in children's educational and school performance. *Journal of Community Psychology* 27, no. 2: 817–839.

Karr, Catherine, and Susan Kline. "Homeless Children: What Every Clinician Should Know." *Pediatrics in Review* 25, no. 7 (2004), 235–241.

Kessler-Sklar, Susan L. and Amy J. Baker. 2000. School District Parent Involvement Policies and Programs. *The Elementary School Journal.* 101, no. 1: 101–121.

Kinnaman, Daniel E. 2002. Meaningful parent involvement: school districts should involve parents as partners and not just supporters. *District Administration.* 38, no. 11: 72.

Kirschenbaum, Howard. 2000. The Principal's View. *High School Magazine* 7, no. 5: 26–29.

Kozol, Jonathan. *The Shame of the Nation: The Restoration of Apartheid Schooling in America.* New York: Crown, 2005.

Kunjufu, Jawanza. 2002. *Black Students, Middle Class Teachers.* Sauk Village, IL: African American Images.

Lawrence-Webb, C, J Okundaye, and G Hafner. 2003. Education and kinship givers: creating a new vision. *Families in Society: The Journal of Contemporary Human Services.* 84, no. 1: 135–143.

Lazares, John. 1999. *Please don't call my mother.* Midlothian, VA: Judy Wood Publishing Company and Consulting Services.

Levy, Maran, Brenda Heffner, Tara Stewart, and Gail Beeman. "The Efficacy of Asthma Case Management in an Urban School District in Reducing School Absences and Hospitalizations for Asthma." *Journal of School Health* 76, no. 6 (2006), 320–324.

Lightfoot, Dory 2004. Some Parents Just Don't Care: Decoding The Meaning of Parental Involvement in Urban Schools. *Urban Education* 39, no 1: 91–107.

McKay, Mary M., Marc S. Atkins, Tracie Hawkins, Catherine Brown, and Cynthia J. Lynn. 2003. African American parental involvement in children's schooling: racial socialization and social support from the parent community. *American Journal of Community Psychology*, 32, no. 1, 107–115.

Marcon, R.A. 1999. Positive relationships between parent school involvement and public school inner-city preschoolers' development and academic performance. *School Psychology Review*, 28, no. 3: 395–412.

Matsui, Elizabeth C. Elinor Simons, Cynthia Rand, Arlene Butz, Timothy J. Buckley, Patrick Breysse, and Peyton A. Eggleston. "Airborne Mouse Allergen in the Homes of Inner-City Children with Asthma." *Journal of Allergy and Clinical Immunology* 115, no. 2 (2005), 358–363.

Miedel, Wendy and Arthur Reynolds. 1999. Parent Involvement in Early Intervention for Disadvantaged Children: Does It Matter? *Journal of School Psychology* 37, no. 4: 379–402.

National Center for Chronic Disease Prevention and Health Promotion – Division of Population Heath (CDC) – Health and Academic Achievement, 2014.

National Center for Education Statistics. 2005. United States Department of Education. Washington, D.C.: Institute of Education Sciences.

National Fatherhood Initiative. *A Guide to Strengthening Fatherhood in Your Community: Moving from Inspiration to Implementation.* Germantown, Maryland: National Fatherhood Initiative, 2011.

National Parent–Teacher Association. 2000.

"New Study Concludes That for Low-Income Blacks, Environmental Experiences Sway Over Genes." *The Journal of Blacks in Higher Education* 20, no. 41 (2003), 96.

No Child Left Behind: Parental Involvement: Title I, Part A - Non-Regulatory Guidance, Department of Education, 2004.

Obama, Barack. State of the Union Address. February 24, 2009.

Ogbu, John. 2003. *Black American Students in an Affluent Suburb: A Study of Academic Disengagement*. Mahwah, NJ: Lawrence Erlbaum Publishers.

Parental Involvement, Title I, Part A. Non-Regulatory Guidance, Department of Education, 2004.

Peressini, Dominic D. 1998. What's all the fuss about involving parents in mathematics education? *Teaching Children Mathematics*. 4, no. 6: 320–326.

Ravitch, Diane. 1983. *The Troubled Crusade: American Education, 1945 – 1980*. New York: Basic Books.

———. 1985. *The Schools We Deserve: Reflections on the Educational Crises of Our Time*. New York: Basic Books.

Ravitch, Diane and Maris A. Vinovskis. 1995. *Learning from the Past: What History Teaches Us About School Reform*. Baltimore: The Johns Hopkins University Press.

Reay, Diane. (1998).Classifying feminist research: exploring the psychological impact of social class on mothers' involvement in children's schooling. *Feminism and Psychology*. 8 (2). 155–171.

Rothman, Nancy, Rita J. Lourie, and John Gaughan. "Lead Awareness: North Philly Style." *American Journal of Public Health* 92, no. 5 (2002), 739–741.

Sanders, Mavis G. 1998. The effects of school, family, and community support on the academic achievement of African American adolescents. *Urban Education*, 33, no. 3: 385–409.

Scheie, David and Mia Robillos 2003. Creating Effective Schools Through Parent and Community Organizing: Two Case Studies of the Hazen Foundation's Public Education Strategy. The Edward W. Hazen Foundation.

Schnoes, Connie, Robert Reid, Mary Wagner, and Camille Marder. "ADHD among Students Receiving Special Education Services: A National Survey." *Exceptional Children* 72 (2006), 483–496.

Smrekar, Claire and Lora Cohen-Vogel. 2001. The voices of parents: rethinking the intersection of family and school. *Peabody Journal of Education*. 76, no. 2: 75–100.

Spring, Joel. 1976. *The Sorting Machine: National Educational Policy since 1945*. New York: David McKay Company.

————. 1994. The American School, 1642 – 1993. New York: McGraw-Hill.

Sterbinsky, Allan and Steven M. Ross. 2003. *School Observation Measure – Reliability Study*. Memphis, TN: The Center for Research in Educational Policy.

Thompson, Gail. (2003). No parent left behind; strengthening ties between educators and African American parents/guardians. *Urban Review*, 35, no. 1: 7–23.

U.S. Public Health Service. 2000. *Report of the Surgeon General's Conference on Children's Mental Health: A National Action Agenda*. Washington, D.C.: Department of Health and Human Services.

Van Cura, Maureen. "The Relationship Between School-Based Health Centers, Rates of Early Dismissal from School, and Loss of Seat Time." *Journal of School Health* 80, no. 8 (2010), 37.

Vassallo, Philip. 2000. More than Grades: How Choice Boots Parental Involvement and Benefits Children. Washington, D.C.: Cato Institute.

Weller, Lawrence, Doren D. Fredrickson, Cindy Burbach, Craign A. Molgaard, Lolem Ngong. 2004. Chronic Disease Medication Administration Rates in a Public School System. *Journal of School Health* 74, no. 5: 161–165.

White, LJ. 1998. National PTA standards for parent/family involvement programs. *High School Magazine*, 5, no. 1: 8–12.